EASIEST MANDOLIN BOOK

By William Bay

1 2 3 4 5 6 7 8 9 0

Tuning the Mandolin

The mandolin is tuned like the violin — the first string E, second string A, third string D, fourth string G. (See diagram below for tuning.) A pitch pipe for the violin may be purchased from any music store. The mandolin has duplicate strings for each pitch. These duplicate strings are tuned in unison.

| 1st String "E" | 3rd String "D" |
| 2nd String "A" | 4th String "G" |

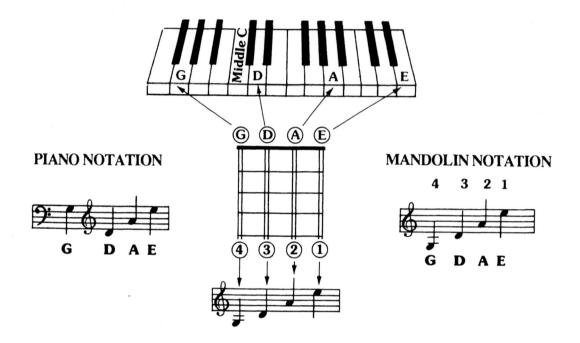

PIANO NOTATION

G   D A E

MANDOLIN NOTATION

4   3   2   1

G   D A E

ANOTHER METHOD OF TUNING

Place the finger behind the seventh fret of the fourth string to obtain the pitch of the third string (D).

Place the finger behind the seventh fret of the third string to obtain the pitch of the second string (A).

Place the finger behind the seventh fret of the second string to obtain the pitch of the first string (E).

PITCH PIPES

Pitch pipes for the mandolin (violin) may be purchased at any music store. Each pipe will have the correct pitch.

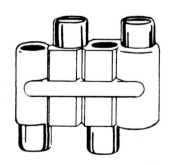

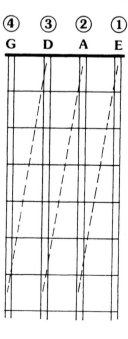

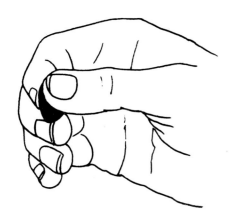

How to Read Chord Symbols

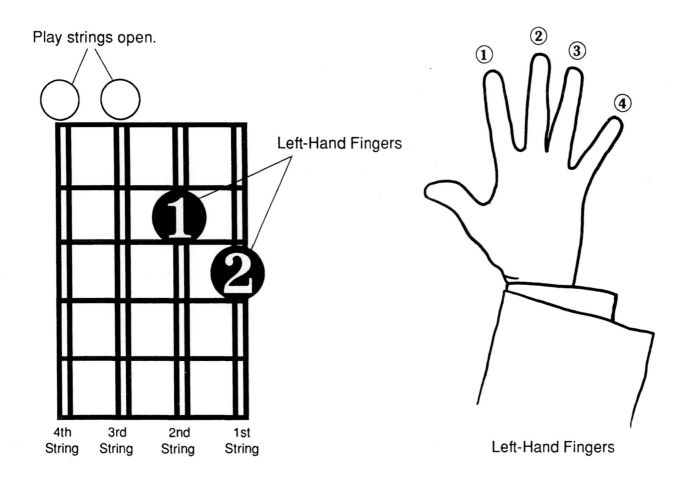

Play strings open.

Left-Hand Fingers

① ② ③ ④

4th String   3rd String   2nd String   1st String

Left-Hand Fingers

Chords in the Key of G

The three primary chords in the key of G are: G, C, and D7.

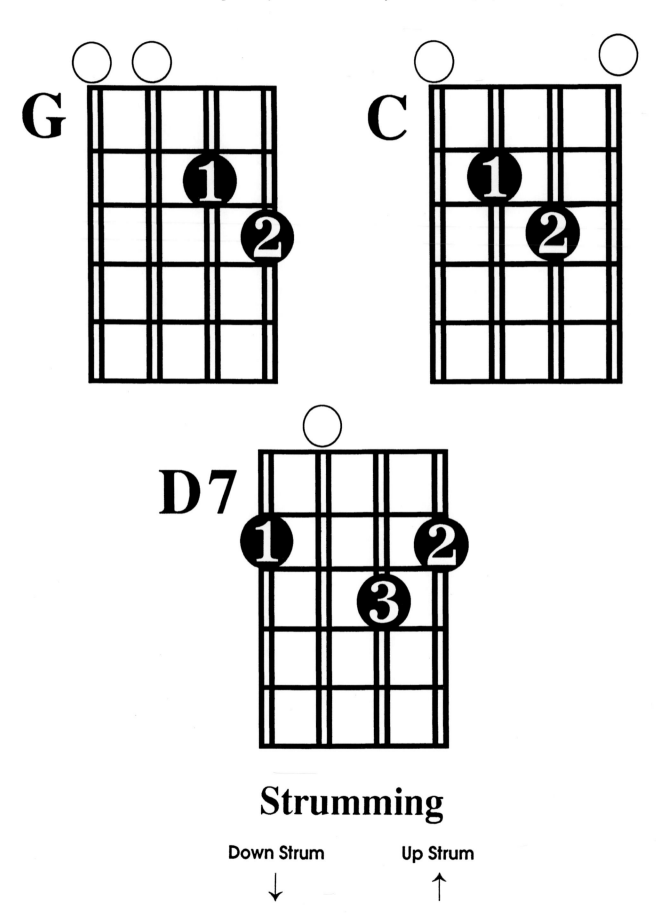

Strumming

Down Strum

↓

Up Strum

↑

Time Signature

$\frac{4}{4}$ or **C** = Common Time

Four strums or beats per measure. Hold the G chord and play in this manner:

$\frac{4}{4}$ **G** ↓ one   ↓ two   ↓ three   ↓ four | **G** ↓ one   ↓ two   ↓ three   ↓ four ‖

$\frac{3}{4}$ = Three-Four or Waltz Time

Three strums or beats per measure. Hold the G chord and play in this manner:

$\frac{3}{4}$ **G** ↓ one   ↓ two   ↓ three | **G** ↓ one   ↓ two   ↓ three ‖

$\frac{2}{4}$ = Two-Four Time

Two strums or beats per measure. Hold the G chord and play in this manner:

$\frac{2}{4}$ **G** ↓ one   ↓ two | **G** ↓ one   ↓ two ‖

$\frac{6}{8}$ = Six-Eight Time

Six strums or beats per measure. Accent beats 1 and 4:

$\frac{6}{8}$ **G** ↓ *one*   ↓ two   ↓ three   ↓ *four*   ↓ five   ↓ six ‖   or try $\frac{6}{8}$ **G** ↓ *one/two*   ↑ three   ↓ *four/five*   ↑ six ‖

5

Brother John

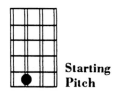

Starting Pitch

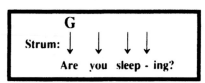

French Round

Moderately

Are you sleep - ing? Are you sleep - ing? Bro - ther John. Bro - ther John.

Morn - ing bells are ring - ing! Morn - ing bells are ring - ing! Din - dan - don. Din - dan - don.

French: Frè-re Jac-ques, Frè-re Jac-ques, Dor-mez vous? Dor-mez vous?

Son-nez-la ma-ti-ne, Son-nez-la ma-ti-ne, Din don din, Din don din.

Rock-A-My Soul

Starting Pitch

Spiritual

Swing Feeling

Rock - a - my soul ___ in the bo - som of A - bra - ham;

Rock - a - my soul ___ in the bo - som of A - bra - ham; Rock - a - my soul ___ in the

bo - som of A - bra - ham; Oh, Rock - a - my soul.

6

Swing Low Sweet Chariot

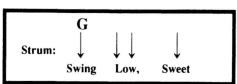

Slowly

Spiritual

Swing low, sweet char-i-ot,___ com-in' for to car-ry me home.

Swing___ low, sweet char-i-ot,___ com-in' for to car-ry me home.

Looked o-ver Jor-dan, what did I see?__ Com-in' for to car-ry me home? A

band___ of an-gels com-in' af-ter me,__ com-in' for to car-ry me home!

Comin' Through The Rye

Slowly

Scotland

If a bod-y meet a bod-y com-in' through the rye,

If a bod-y kiss a bod-y, need a bod-y cry?

Ev-'ry las-sie has a lad-die, none, they say, have I, yet

all the lads they smile on me, when com-in' through the Rye.

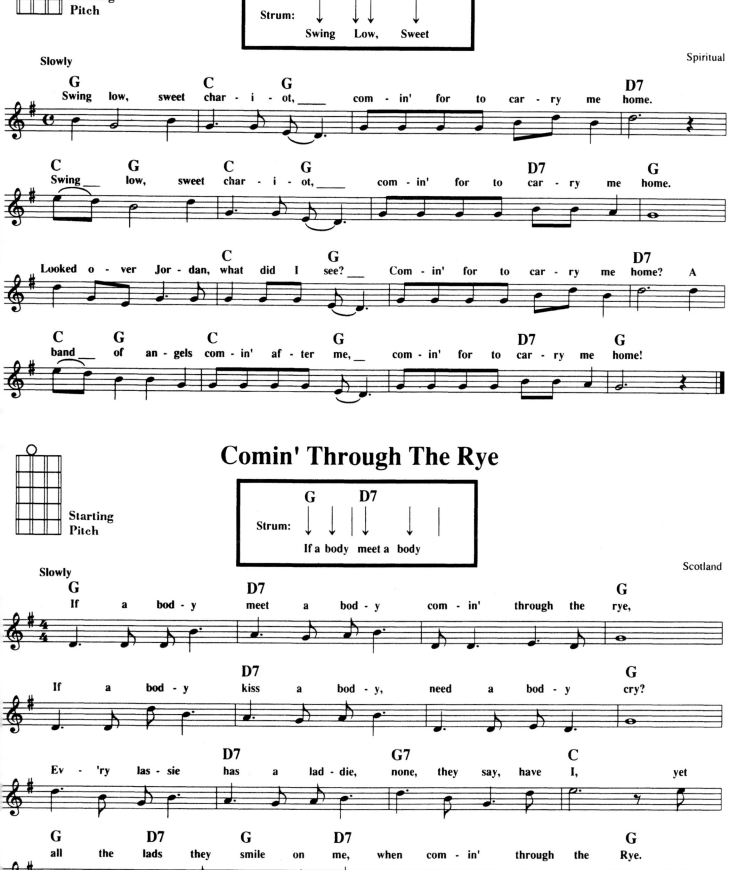

The Foggy, Foggy Dew

2. One night she knelt close by my side
As I lay fast asleep.
She threw her arms around my neck,
And then began to weep.
She wept, she cried, she tore her hair,
Ah me, what could I do?
So all night long I held her in my arms,
Just to keep her from the foggy, foggy dew.

3. Oh, I am a bachelor, I live with my son,
We work at the weaver's trade.
And every single time I look into his eyes
He reminds me of the fair young maid.
He reminds me of the winter time,
And of the summer too.
And the many, many times I held her in my arms,
Just to keep her from the foggy, foggy dew.

Peace Like A River

2. I've got joy like a fountain

3. I've got love like an ocean.

8

The Bold Fisherman

Sea Song

2. "Good morning brother fisherman, what brings you down this way?
"I come to court some lady gay from o'er the rolling sea,
From o'er the rolling sea,
I come to court some lady gay from o'er the rolling sea.

Sourwood Mountain

American Folk Song

2. My true love's a blue eyed daisy...
   If she won't marry me I'll go crazy...

3. My true love up on the hill...
   If she won't marry me her sister will...

4. My true love's a sun burnt daisy
   She won't work and I'm too lazy.

9

The Wee Cooper O'Fife

Scotland

2. She wouldna bake, she wouldna brew;
   For the spoilin' o' her homely hue...

3. She wouldna card, she wouldna spin...
   For the shamin' o' her gentle kin...

4. She wouldna wash, she wouldna wring...
   For the spoilin' o' her golden ring...

5. The cooper has gone to his wool pack...
   He laid a sheep skin across his wife's back...

6. I wouldna thrash ye for your gentle kin...
   But I will thrash my own sheep skin...

7. A'ye wha hae gotten a gentle wife...
   Send ye for the Wee Cooper O'Fife...

All Through The Night

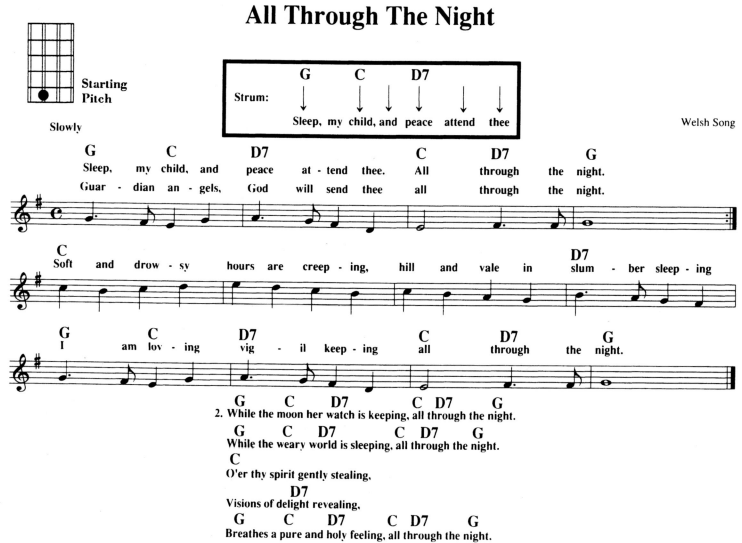

Welsh Song

2. While the moon her watch is keeping, all through the night.
While the weary world is sleeping, all through the night.
O'er thy spirit gently stealing,
Visions of delight revealing,
Breathes a pure and holy feeling, all through the night.

10

The Wabash Cannonball

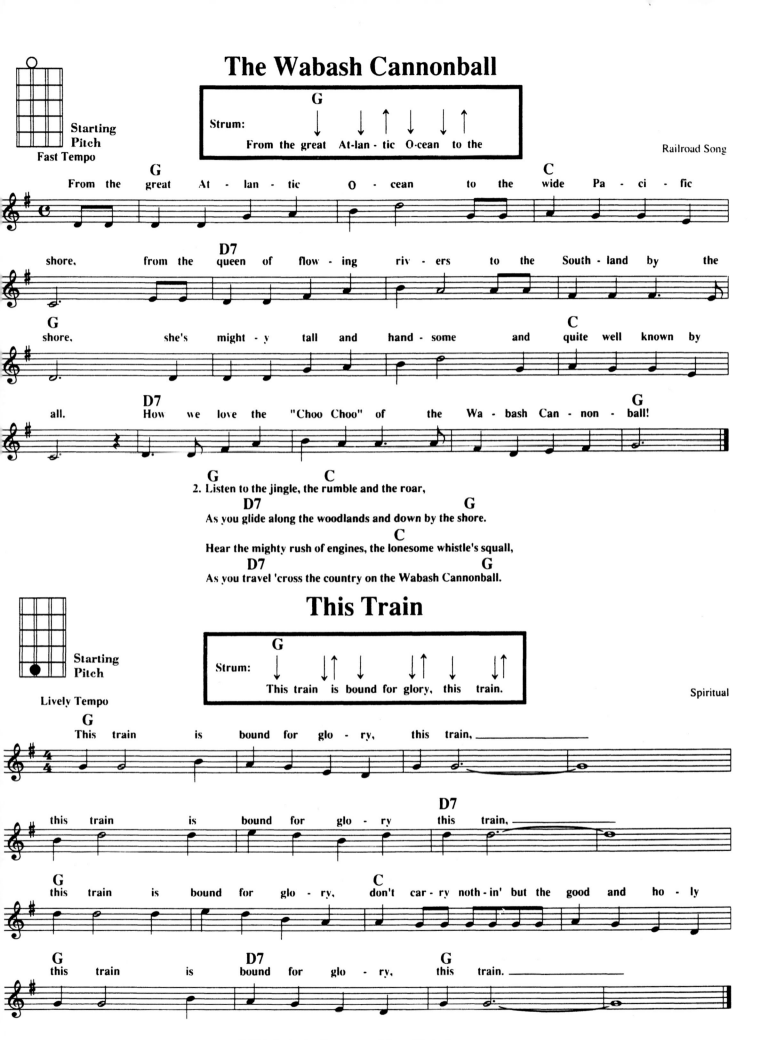

Railroad Song

Starting Pitch
Fast Tempo

Strum: G — From the great At-lan-tic O-cean to the

From the great At-lan-tic O-cean to the wide Pa-ci-fic shore, from the queen of flow-ing riv-ers to the South-land by the shore, she's might-y tall and hand-some and quite well known by all. How we love the "Choo Choo" of the Wa-bash Can-non-ball!

2.
G   **C**
Listen to the jingle, the rumble and the roar,
D7   **G**
As you glide along the woodlands and down by the shore.
     C
Hear the mighty rush of engines, the lonesome whistle's squall,
D7   **G**
As you travel 'cross the country on the Wabash Cannonball.

This Train

Spiritual

Starting Pitch
Lively Tempo

Strum: G — This train is bound for glory, this train.

This train is bound for glo-ry, this train, this train is bound for glo-ry this train, this train is bound for glo-ry, don't car-ry noth-in' but the good and ho-ly this train is bound for glo-ry, this train.

2. This train don't carry gamblers, this train . . .
3. This train is for rejoicing! This train . . .

11

La Cucaracha

Mexican

The Sloop "John B."

Calypso

2. So hoist up the John B. sails, see how the main-sail set,
Send for the captain ashore let me go home.
Let me go home, let me go home. I
Feel so break up I wanna go home.

Chords in the Key of D

The three primary chords in the key of D are: D, G, and A7.

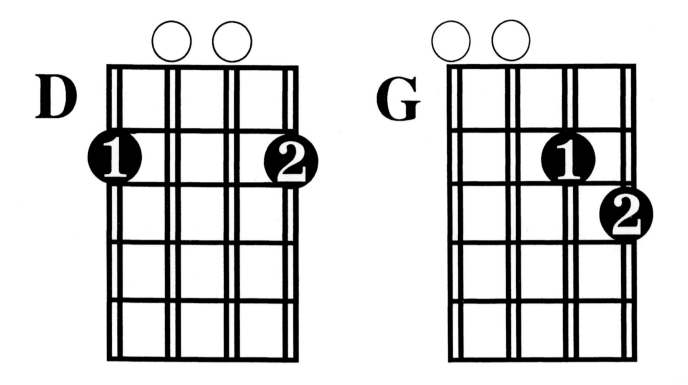

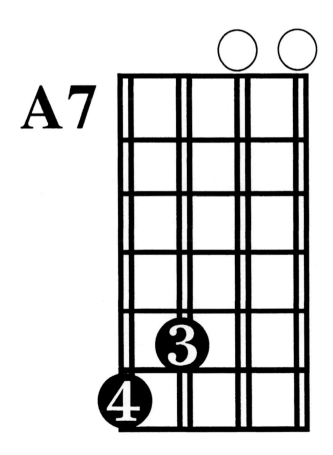

He's Got The Whole World

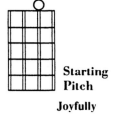

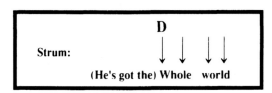

Starting Pitch

Joyfully

Spiritual

2. He's got the little bitty baby
in His hands.
He's got the whole world
in His hands.

3. He got you and me brother,
in His hands
He got the whole world in
His hands.

4. He's got the wind and the rain
in his hands
He's got the whole world
in his hands.

Sail Away Ladies

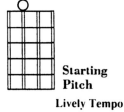

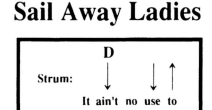

Starting Pitch

Lively Tempo

Sea Song

D
2. I've got a hone in Tennessee
A7 D
Sail away ladies, sail away.
That's the place I wanna be,
A7 D
Sail away ladies, sail away. *(CHO.)*

D
3. If ever I get my new house done,
A7 D
Sail away ladies, sail away.
I'll give the old one to my son,
A7 D
Sail away ladies, sail away. *(CHO.)*

D
4. Come along boys, and go with me,
A7 D
Sail away ladies, sail away.
We'll go down to Tennessee,
A7 D
Sail away ladies, sail away.

D
5. Ever I get my new house done,
A7   D
Love you, pretty girls, one by one.
Hush little baby don't you cry
A7 D
You'll be an angel by and by.

Lord Lovel

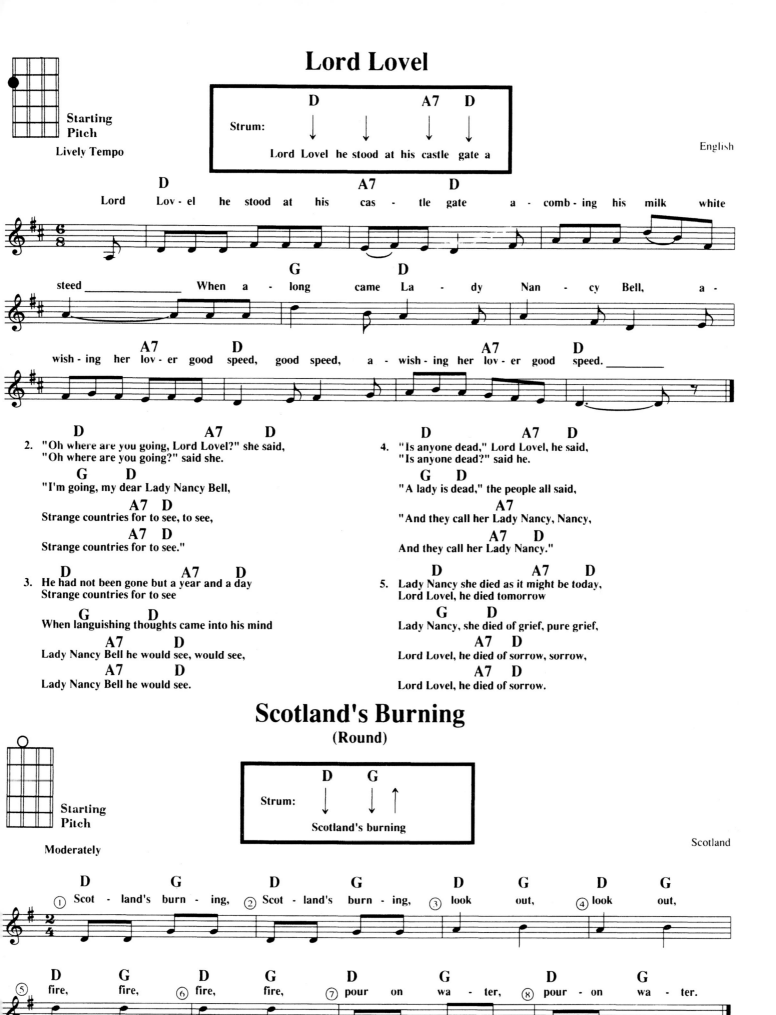

Starting Pitch
Lively Tempo

English

Strum:

D   A7   D

Lord Lovel he stood at his castle gate a

D   **A7**   **D**

Lord Lov-el he stood at his cas - tle gate a - comb-ing his milk white

G   **D**

steed _____ When a - long came La - dy Nan - cy Bell, a -

A7   **D**   **A7**   **D**

wish - ing her lov - er good speed, good speed, a - wish - ing her lov - er good speed. _____

     D   **A7**   **D**
2. "Oh where are you going, Lord Lovel?" she said,
"Oh where are you going?" said she.
     G   **D**
"I'm going, my dear Lady Nancy Bell,
     A7   **D**
Strange countries for to see, to see,
     A7   **D**
Strange countries for to see."

    D   **A7**   **D**
3. He had not been gone but a year and a day
Strange countries for to see
     G   **D**
When languishing thoughts came into his mind
     A7   **D**
Lady Nancy Bell he would see, would see,
     A7   **D**
Lady Nancy Bell he would see.

     D   **A7**   **D**
4. "Is anyone dead," Lord Lovel, he said,
"Is anyone dead?" said he.
     G   **D**
"A lady is dead," the people all said,
     A7
"And they call her Lady Nancy, Nancy,
     A7   **D**
And they call her Lady Nancy."

     D   **A7**   **D**
5. Lady Nancy she died as it might be today,
Lord Lovel, he died tomorrow
     G   **D**
Lady Nancy, she died of grief, pure grief,
     A7   **D**
Lord Lovel, he died of sorrow, sorrow,
     A7   **D**
Lord Lovel, he died of sorrow.

Scotland's Burning
(Round)

Starting Pitch
Moderately

Scotland

Strum:

D   G

Scotland's burning

D   **G**   **D**   **G**   **D**   **G**   **D**   **G**
① Scot - land's burn - ing, ② Scot - land's burn - ing, ③ look out, ④ look out,

D   **G**   **D**   **G**   **D**   **G**   **D**   **G**
⑤ fire, fire, ⑥ fire, fire, ⑦ pour on wa - ter, ⑧ pour - on wa - ter.

15

Rise And Shine
[Noah]

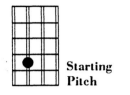

Starting Pitch

Rousing Tempo

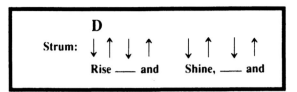

D

Strum: ↓ ↑ ↓ ↑   ↓ ↑ ↓ ↑

Rise —— and   Shine, —— and

Bible Song

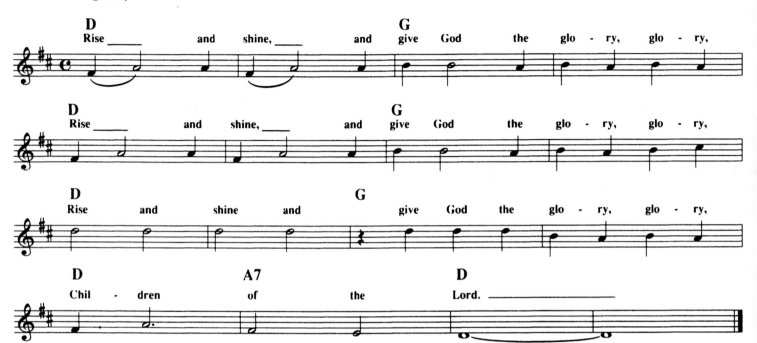

D   G
Rise ____ and shine, ____ and give God the glo - ry, glo - ry,

D   G
Rise ____ and shine, ____ and give God the glo - ry, glo - ry,

D   G
Rise and shine and give God the glo - ry, glo - ry,

D   A7   D
Chil - dren of the Lord. _____

    D   G
2. The Lord said, "Noah, there's gonna be a floody, floody."

   D   G
The Lord said, "Noah, there's gonna be a floody, floody."

D   G
Get your children out of the muddy, muddy!"

D A7 D
Children of the Lord.

    D   G
3. Noah, he built him, he built him an arky, arky,

   D   G
Noah, he built him, he built him an arky, arky,

D   G
Made it out of hickory barky, barky,

D A7 D
Children of the Lord.

    D   G
4. The animals, they came, they came by twosy, twosy,

   D   G
The animals, they came, they came by twosy, twosy,

D   G
Elephants and kangaroosy, roosy.

D A7 D
Children of the Lord.

    D   G
5. It rained and rained for forty daysy, daysy,

   D   G
It rained and rained for forty daysy, daysy,

D   G
Drove those animals nearly crazy, crazy,

D A7 D
Children of the Lord.

    D   G
6. The sun came out and dried up the landy, landy,

   D   G
The sun came out and dried up the landy, landy,

D   G
Everyone felt fine and dandy, dandy,

D A7 D
Children of the Lord. *Repeat first verse*

Come And Go With Me

Spiritual

2. There ain't no bowing in that land, ain't no bowing in that land,
Ain't no bowing in that land where I'm bound.
There ain't no bowing in that land, ain't no bowing in that land,
Ain't no bowing in that land where I'm bound.

3. There ain't no kneeling in that land, ain't no kneeling in that land,
Ain't no kneeling in that land where I'm bound.
There ain't no kneeling in that land, ain't no kneeling in that land,
Ain't no kneeling in that land where I'm bound.

4. There's peace and freedom in that land, peace and freedom in that land,
Peace and freedom in that land where I'm bound.
There's peace and freedom in that land, peace and freedom in that land,
Peace and freedom in that land where I'm bound.

Old Joe Clark

Southern Banjo Song

Strum:
D
I used to live on a mountain top.

Lively Tempo

D
I used to live on a moun-tain top. Now I live in town I'm

stay-ing at the big ho-tel, court-in' Bet-sey Brown.   C   D

Chrous
Fare ye well, old Joe Clark, fare ye well I'm bound,   C

fare ye well, old Joe Clark, good-bye Bet-sey Brown.   C   D

D
2. Old Joe Clark, the preacher's son,

Preached all over the plain,

The only text he ever knew

            C   D
Was "high, low jack and the game."

Chorus

D
3. Old Joe Clark had a mule,

His name was Morgan Brown,

'And every tooth in that mule's head

        C D
Was sixteen inches around.

Chorus

D
4. Old Joe Clark had a house

Fifteen stories high

And every story in that house

        C D
Was filled with chicken pie.

Chorus

D
5. I went down to old Joe's house

He invited me to supper,

I stumped my toe on the table leg

        C   D
And stuck my nose in the butter.

Chorus

Oh! Susanna

Betty And Dupree

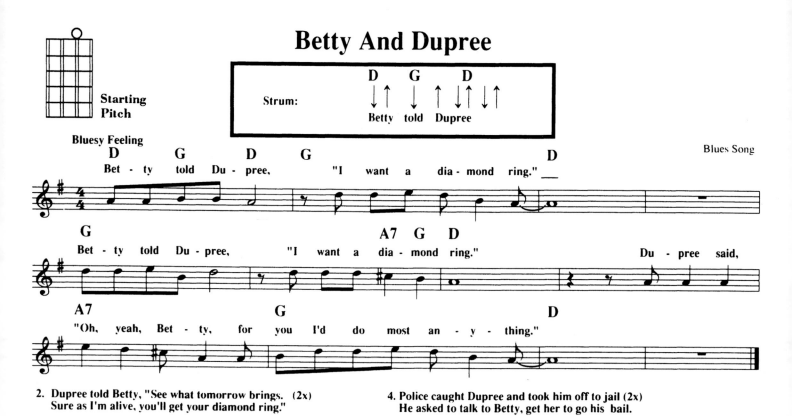

2. Dupree told Betty, "See what tomorrow brings. (2x)
   Sure as I'm alive, you'll get your diamond ring."

3. Dupree had a pistol, it was a forty-four (2x)
   Stuck it in his pocket, stuck up a jewelry store.

4. Police caught Dupree and took him off to jail (2x)
   He asked to talk to Betty, get her to go his bail.

5. Betty told Dupree, "I want to see your face. (2x)
   You know I love you baby, but I just can't take your place."

Believe Me If All Those Endearing Young Charms

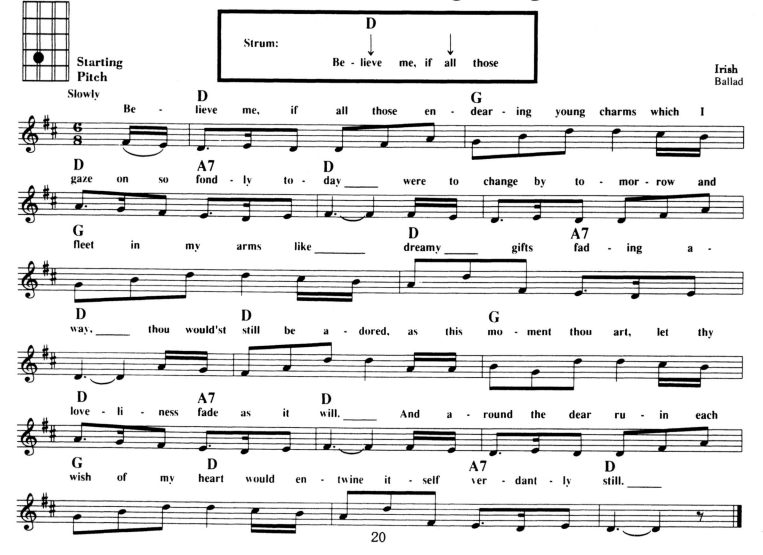

Turkey In The Straw

American Fiddle Tune

2. Oh, I went out to milk and I didn't know how,
I milked a goat instead of a cow.
A monkey sitting on a pile of straw,
A-winkin' his eyes at his mother-in-law.
Chorus

3. Met Mr. Catfish comin' down stream,
Says Mr. Catfish, "What does you mean?"
Caught Mr. Catfish by the snout
And turned Mr. Catfish wrong side out
Chorus

4. Came to the river and I couldn't get across
Paid five dollars for an old blind hoss
Wouldn't go ahead, nor he wouldn't stand still
So he went up and down like an old saw mill.
Chorus

5. As I came down the new cut road
Met Mr. Bullfrog, met Miss Toad
And every time Miss Toad would sing
Ole Bullfrog cut a pigeon wing.
Chorus

6. O I jumped in the seat, and I gave a little yell
The horses run away, broke the wagon all to hell;
Sugar in the gourd and honey in the horn,
I never was so happy since the hour I was born.
Chorus

21

Reading Tablature

The mandolin consists of eight strings, with each pair tuned in unison. In tablature, only one line is used to represent both strings. Tablature is simply a drawing of four lines to represent these strings. Numbers are given to show the musician either to pick the open strings or in which fret he or she is to press down to produce the required note.

```
1st String ————————————————————————————————————— 1
2nd String ————————————————————————————————————— 2
3rd String ————————————————————————————————————— 3
4th String ————————————————————————————————————— 4
```

The numbers placed on the tablature

lines show which fret to press

down with the left-hand

fingers.

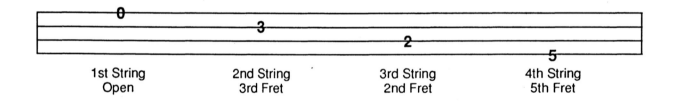

1st String	2nd String	3rd String	4th String
Open	3rd Fret	2nd Fret	5th Fret

When two or more notes are

to be played at the same time,

they are shown as follows:

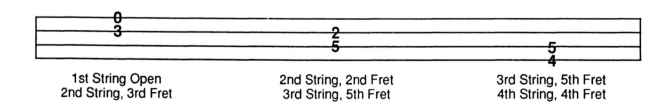

1st String Open	2nd String, 2nd Fret	3rd String, 5th Fret
2nd String, 3rd Fret	3rd String, 5th Fret	4th String, 4th Fret

Solos

TYPES OF NOTES

 The type of note will indicate the length of its sound.

○ This is a whole note.

4 beats
A whole note will receive 4 beats or counts.

♩ This is a half note.

2 beats
A half note will receive 2 beats or counts.

♩ This is a quarter note.

1 beat
A quarter note will receive 1 beat or count.

♪ This is an eighth note.

½ beat
An eighth note will receive ½ beat or count (2 for 1 beat).

♬ This is a sixteenth note.

¼ beat — 4 per beat

RESTS

A **rest** is a sign that designates a period of silence.
This period of silence will be of the same duration as the note to which it corresponds.

𝄾 This is an eighth rest.

𝄿 This is a sixteenth rest.

▬ This is a half rest. Note that it lies on the line.

▬ This is a whole rest. Note that it hangs down from the line.

𝄽 This is a quarter rest.

NOTES

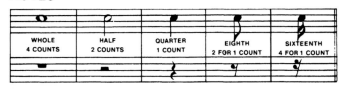

WHOLE 4 COUNTS	HALF 2 COUNTS	QUARTER 1 COUNT	EIGHTH 2 FOR 1 COUNT	SIXTEENTH 4 FOR 1 COUNT

RESTS

It Ain't Gonna Rain

∏ = Down Pick
V = Up Pick

23

Oh, Them Golden Slippers

Ground Hog

Bury Me Beneath The Willow

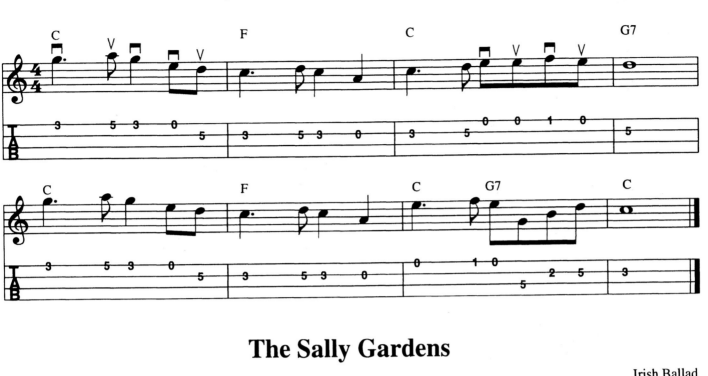

The Sally Gardens

Irish Ballad

Black-Eyed Susie

The Black Velvet Band

Irish Ballad

Old Rosin, The Beau

Crossing Over To Ireland

This Little Light Of Mine

The Wreck Of The Old 97

Arkansas Traveler

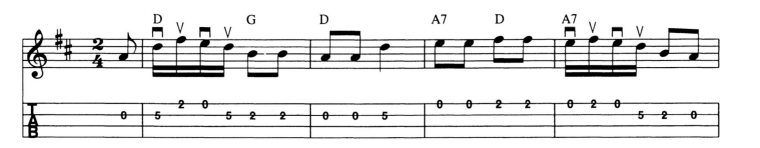

Filimiooriay

The Major Chords
(Symbol C, F, Etc.)

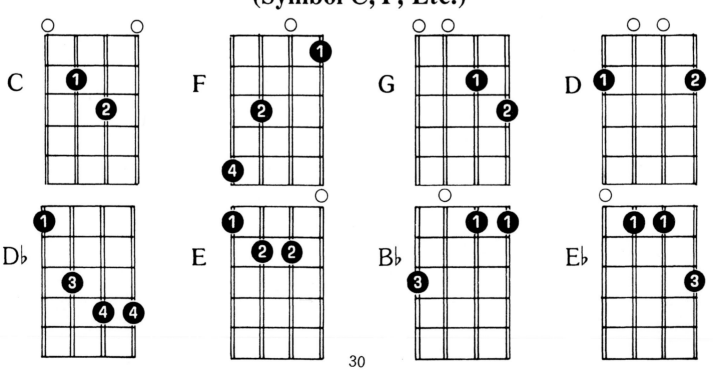

The Major Chords
(cont.)

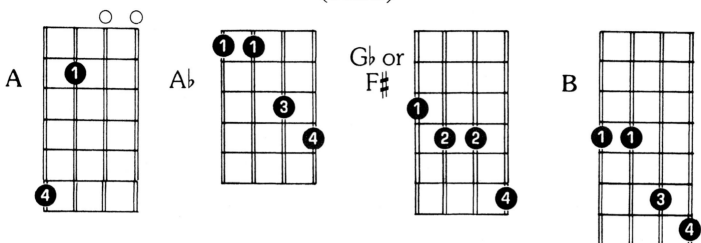

A   A♭   G♭ or F♯   B

The Dominant Seventh Chords
(Symbol C7, F7, Etc.)

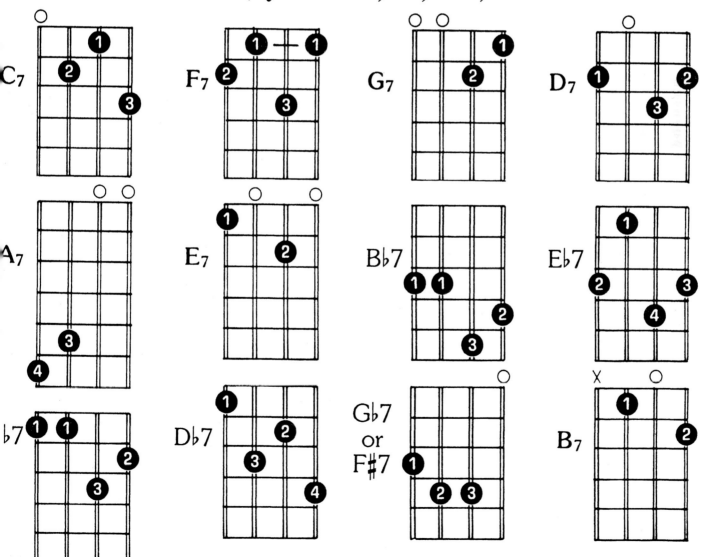

C7   F7   G7   D7

A7   E7   B♭7   E♭7

♭7   D♭7   G♭7 or F♯7   B7

31

The Minor Chords
(Symbol Cm, Fm, Etc.)

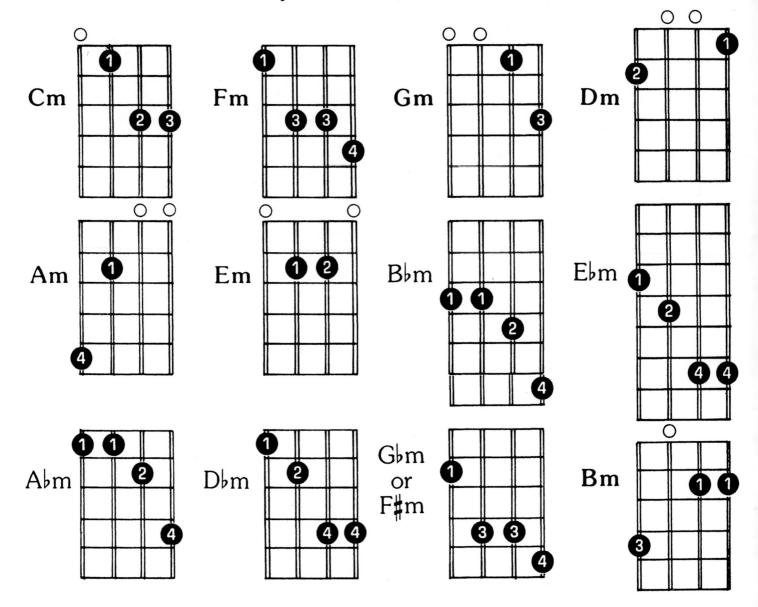

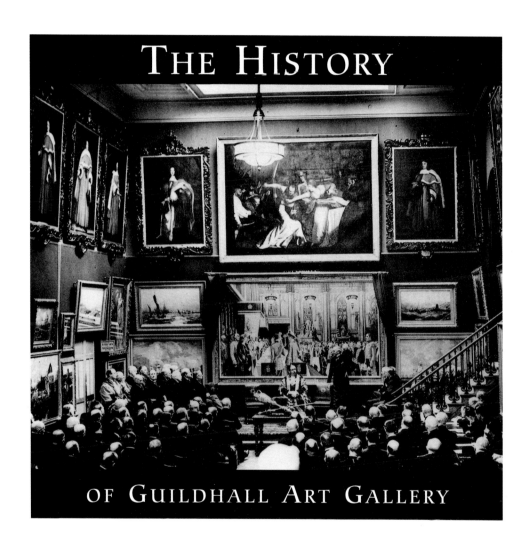

THE HISTORY

OF GUILDHALL ART GALLERY

ACKNOWLEDGEMENTS

This book draws on information contained in the minutes and papers of the Library Committee, the City Lands Committee, the Guildhall Reconstruction Committee and the Court of Common Council, held by the Corporation of London Records Office to whose Archivist and staff I am extremely grateful for help and advice. Other details were drawn from Sir Alfred Temple's memoir 'Guildhall Memories' published in 1918. Some details of the wartime storage arrangements and the post war reassembling of the collections are contained in a typescript record held in Guildhall Library known colloquially as 'The Bible', while others come from the CLRO. Guildhall Library holds *The Times*, *The City Press* and the *Art Journal* from which information about the City of London Art Society was derived. I am very grateful to my Guildhall Library colleagues in both the Printed Books and Prints and Maps sections for their patient assistance with my enquiries. The late Mr J L Howgego communicated very helpful details about the appearance of the Gallery in the 1930s, shortly before his death in 1996, and Mrs E Bromley, wife of the late Mr John Bromley, gave her kind permission for the inclusion of her husband's account of the night of May 10 1941, which is lodged in Guildhall Library.

ISBN 1-902795-00-8

Cover: Gallery I furnished for a reception, c.1930 (?), with Copley's *Defeat of the Floating Batteries* at the East end. (Guildhall Library, Prints and Maps Collection)

Title page: Unveiling ceremony in March 1939 of
The Coronation Luncheon at Guildhall, 1937 by Frank Salisbury.
(Guildhall Library, Prints and Maps Collection)

Back cover: The Great Hall after the raid of December 29 1940: view from the Guildhall Porch (Guildhall Library, Prints and Maps Collection)

Published by Guildhall Art Gallery, 1999
Designed by Mick Keates
Produced by Supreme Publishing Services

Façade of Guildhall Art Gallery, showing its entrance (beside the step ladder) adjoining the Porch, 1896.

Guildhall Library, Prints and Maps Collection

'WHEN IN THE YEAR 1886, the Corporation took the important step of [...] creating its own Art Gallery, it added to itself the task of supporting, encouraging and developing this new venture, so that it should ultimately form a Collection of Art Treasures worthy of the capital city of the Empire – a Collection which eventually should be housed in a building which the merits of such Pictures demanded, specially planned for the requirements of a modern Art Gallery, and architecturally something of which the City of London might be proud'.

So reported the Corporation of London's Library Committee to the Court of Common Council in 1925, arguing its case for the long overdue rebuilding of the Art Gallery at Guildhall. But the Gallery was not rebuilt, and sixteen years later the War wiped out even the old inadequate premises. Since 1941 its collection has been dispersed among assorted stores and borrowers. Only now are the hopes of those long-ago Committee members triumphantly realised in the new Guildhall Art Gallery – the first purpose-built and permanent home for the Corporation of London's collection of works of art

When the City of London Fine Art Gallery – usually known as Guildhall Art Gallery – first opened its doors to the public on June 24 1886, it owed its existence to the efforts of several individuals – notably Library Committe members Henry Clarke and George Shaw – and to two important factors. The first was the recent establishment in several major cities

Sir Francis Wyatt Truscott,
Lord Mayor, 1880.
*Guildhall Library, Prints and
Maps Collection*

Charles Bell Birch (1832-1893):
Marble bust of Sir Francis
Wyatt Truscott, 1881. Birch
was an active member of the
City of London Society of
Artists. The Society presented
this bust of himself to Truscott
at the Mansion House in
January 1882.
Guildhall Art Gallery

of large municipal museums and art galleries, to which the publicly acclaimed commitment of the Corporations of those cities made the Corporation of London feel it was being left behind; and secondly the efforts of the City of London Society of Artists, whose exhibition in 1884 at Guildhall was a popular and critical success that demonstrated to the Corporation the level of support that such a venture would receive.

The City of London Society of Artists had been formed in the 1870s by Birmingham landscape painter Bernard Walter Evans (1843-1922) after a meeting of artists at the St John's Wood home of another landscape painter, Nathaniel Green. It had many similarities with the older Royal Birmingham Society of Artists, of which Evans was also a member, sharing with it the aims of exhibiting and selling members' work, providing art education and of establishing a permanent Art Gallery and Academy in suitable purchased or leased premises. The Skinners Company lent its hall for the Society's first exhibition, which was opened by the Lord Mayor and the Society's president, Sir Francis Wyatt Truscott in March 1880. Further exhibitions were held at the hall until 1883; while in March 1882 the Corporation's Curator of Works of Art, J R Dicksee, was one of the organisers of an exhibition and *conversazione* at the Mansion House. The event was held to promote the Society's appeal to the Corporation for help in furthering their aims. It was arranged jointly with the Society for the Encouragement of the Arts and was hosted by the Lord Mayor, who was currently President of the former society and vice-president of the latter.

Perhaps it was Dicksee who suggested in December 1883 that the Society should petition the Court of Common Council to hold their next annual exhibition in the vacated Court of Queen's Bench. This occupied, together with the Court of Common Pleas, a building erected in 1823 on the site of the mediaeval Guildhall Chapel and Blackwell Hall. The Court referred the matter to the City Lands Committee, who agreed that improvements to the lighting of the vacated portion should be made under the direction of the Corporation's Architect, Horace Jones. (Alterations were also made to the stairs, but the Committee turned down the Society's further requests for baize, potted palms and a separate refreshment room.) When their exhibition was opened on May 20 1884 by the Lord Mayor, it comprised 900 works in four rooms. One room was devoted to watercolours, including a drawing of a bascule bridge by Horace Jones which, according to *The Times*, 'calls to mind a question that has long been discussed [...] namely communication across the Thames below London Bridge', and which may have been an early design for his Tower Bridge of 1894. An entire wall of the Gallery was filled with works by Birmingham painters, while Sir Frederic Leighton, the President of the Royal Academy, was among the notable London artists included. On June 27, a *conversazione* was held, during which, reported

George C Maunde (fl. from 1852): Guildhall Museum with an Exhibition of a Portion of the Gardner Collection at the Opening of the New Library 1872.

watercolour; Guildhall Library, Prints and Maps

Charles Bell Birch (1832-1893): Marble bust of Sir Horace Jones, City Architect, 1886, bequeathed by his daughter, Miss A C Jones in 1969.

Guildhall Art Gallery

The Times the following day, 'members of the Savage Club contributed to the enjoyment of the guests with songs, recitations, and some amusing performances. Among those who took part in this entertainment were [...] Mr Charles Bertram, whose card trick illusions as usual greatly puzzled and delighted the spectators'.

By this time, the Society was styling itself 'The City of London Society of Artists and Guildhall Academy of Art'. The success of their exhibition prompted them to petition the City Lands Committee to extend it beyond its scheduled closing date of August 31 until the end of September. However, any assumptions the Society may have made about future support were unfounded. At the eventual end of the exhibition the Committee allowed them a further extension of time until October 18 'upon the distinct understanding that the Society will give up possession of the Courts on that day', but refused their petition to be allowed to use the Court during the autumn and winter for art classes. In March 1885 their application to hold another exhibition was also turned down.

The Society's request was refused because the Corporation had intended to adapt the Court for use by the Clerks in the Chamberlain's Office, in lieu of their existing accommodation 'in which they dreaded passing another Summer and Winter'. Unfortunately for the Clerks this plan was now suspended. Reviewing the Society's exhibition, *The Times* had noted that 'the law courts [...] having been converted into spacious and handsome galleries, [...] it is hoped that these galleries will hereafter be permanently reserved for exhibitions and art classes'. It was this space which Library Committee members Henry Clarke and George Shaw had in mind when they proposed that there should be a permanent art gallery to the Court of Common Council meeting on 30 April 1885. It was accordingly referred back to the Library Committee 'to consider the desirability and practicality of establishing a City of London Art Gallery for the reception and exhibition of works belonging to the Corporation'. On July 30 the Library Committee reported back to the Court in encouraging terms:

'It appears to your Committee that the Paintings, Busts and Engravings at Guildhall, would of themselves form the nucleus of a Gallery of no ordinary interest, and it may reasonably be anticipated that, if the proposed Gallery were established, valuable contributions by way of gift or bequest would from time to time be received. Seeing that other Corporations such as Liverpool, Manchester, Leeds &c., have adopted a course similar to that now contemplated, and have established Galleries that have proved eminently successful, it appears to us that a Gallery in connection with the Corporation of London would, in the increased taste for Art now prevalent, be exceedingly attractive and instructive, especially if the Corporation become, as is very probable, the recipient of such

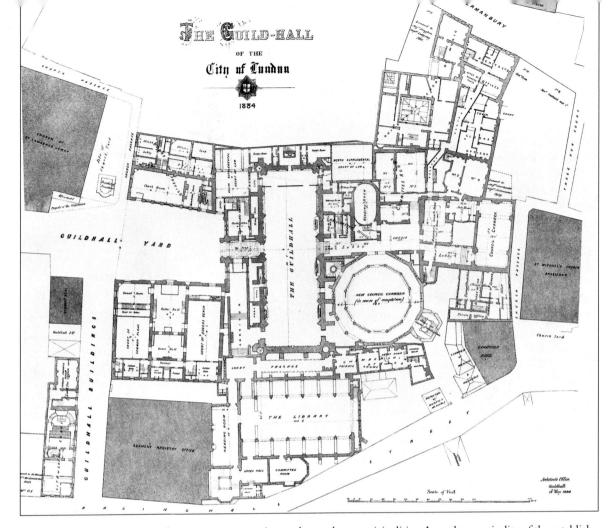

The Guildhall of the City of London: plan dated 19 May 1884, showing the relative positions of the Library and the block containing the Court of Queen's Bench and the Court of Common Pleas which was later to house the new City of London Fine Art Gallery.

Corporation of London Records Office

bequests or presentations as have other municipalities. As to the practicality of the establishment of the Gallery, we deemed it expedient to turn our attention to securing some accommodation of a temporary character for the organisation of the Gallery, and for this purpose we conferred with the City Lands Committee, and subsequently with the Special Guildhall Improvement Committee, and beg now to state that both these Committees expressed their approval of the suggestions and recommendations of your Committee, and their willingness to place at our disposal the vacated Court of Queen's Bench in front of the Guildhall. This Court, being lighted from the Roof, is in our opinion well adapted for the purpose, and is of sufficient size to answer the requirements of a temporary Gallery, and could be adequately fitted up for a sum not exceeding 200L. [...] In conclusion we beg to suggest that in the Reference now in course of consideration by the Special Guildhall Improvement Committe for the re-arrangement of the various Courts and Offices at Guildhall, they be empowered to provide such space on the Upper Floors, or elsewhere, as may be suitable for the purposes of a permanent Art Gallery'.

The City of London Society of Artists had made some alterations to the Court at their own cost, and they were now reimbursed a sum of £150 in respect of these. Further improvements completed by the end of December 1885 by the City Architect included the cutting of a new stair at the entrance giving access to the raised floor of the Gallery, and distempering the walls. In the following March he was instructed to cover the floor and stairs with crimson carpet, and the main thoroughfares with Corticene (a material similar to linoleum), and to provide suitable furniture for the office of the newly appointed Secretary of the Art Gallery.

Plan of the Mayor's Court Offices, 1889. The Gallery occupied the area on the first floor over the Library bookstore, and was reached by stairs from the entrance (bottom left).

Corporation of London Record Office

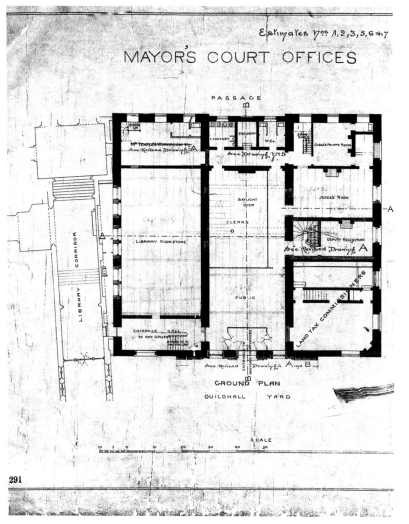

It was envisaged that while the works of art remaining elsewhere at Guildhall would remain in the care of the Curator, J R Dicksee, who had been appointed in 1880 by the City Lands Comittee, those removed to the Art Gallery would be the responsibility of the new Secretary. However, little thought had been given to how the existing Curator would be affected by the new Gallery and the removal to its walls of the best paintings and sculptures for which he had hitherto been responsible, a list of which had already been made and appended to the Library Committee's report. Dicksee discovered the plans to appoint a Secretary for the Gallery in October 1885, and wrote plaintively to the Library Committee to point out that although he reported to the City Lands Committee he had often acted for the former in having pictures hanging in the Library restored and in advising on the purchase of works, concluding 'I have, from the first, had in view the enlargement and proper housing of the Collection and have done all I could to this end, and I think it would be very hard, now fruition is at hand, that I should be superceded'. In fact it was not until December that the Library Committee ordered a report on the appointment of a Secretary to be presented to the Court of Common Council, and on December 16 Dicksee wrote again, this time in application for the new post: 'I understand that a proposal to appoint a Secretary to the new Art Gallery is to be made to the Court tomorrow; I do not know how this may affect me. I am at present engaged on a revised and extended Catalogue by order of the City Lands Committee; so I imagine I am performing one of the chief duties of a Secretary'. But Dicksee must have eliminated himself from the contest by his concluding remark that he would be 'very pleased' to undertake the Secretary's duties in addition to those of Curator (not to mention those as art master at the City of London School). The Library Committee were specific that the appointee should devote himself to Gallery duties alone.

Dicksee's application was considered by the Library Committee together with five others on December 18. The other candidates included Mr Albert Simpson aged 23 (whose application consisted chiefly in stating that he was well known to several Aldermen and Common Councilmen) and a Mr Lyle whose application has not survived: both were immediately struck from the list. There is no record in Committee minutes or papers about any debate as to the suitability of Dicksee or Mr John Day, formerly a fine art printer. Two candidates who were present were called in for interview. Mr Carew Martin was the grandson of the artist John Martin and son of the portrait painter Charles Martin. He had studied in Paris and spoke French, Italian and German; he was well connected with artists, critics and scholars, one uncle – Joseph Bonomi – having been Curator of Sir John Soane's Museum, and another – E H Corbould – having been a drawing master to the Royal Family. His excellent testimonials were from Charles Eastlake, Keeper of the National Gallery, and George Bullen, Keeper of Printed Books at the British Museum. Perhaps Mr Martin seemed too glittering and ambitious to the Library Committee. Their unanimous choice fell on Mr Alfred George Temple.

If it was to Truscott, Clarke and Shaw that the Gallery owed its existence, it would be to Alfred Temple that it owed its phenomenal early success. Aged 37, he had been in the Corporation's service for 17 years as a minuting clerk in the Town Clerk's Office. In that period his salary had increased through promotion from £50 per annum to £325; nevertheless, he accepted his new position at a salary of only £200. (In 1890 it went up again to £300.) Temple had explained in his letter of application that he had long devoted his leisure hours to painting, while he had also studied the history of art and art criticism and had acquainted himself 'with the best works of both the Old and Modern Schools'; and he continued: 'The Appointment I have now the honour to hold, with whatever prospect of advancement there may be, I would readily relinquish for the post of Director [the word 'Secretary' has been crossed out] of your Gallery – and (as I have privately intimated to the Chairman and to a few Members of your Committee) for whatever Honorarium your Committee might think fit to award. Should I be honoured with the appointment I would devote my time and knowledge to your service and nothing should be wanting on my part which could, in any way, contribute to make the proposed Gallery worthy of the Corporation'.

The Committee members must have felt comfortable with this enthusiastic and able man, who had the additional advantage of understanding the workings of the Corporation. They immediately instructed Temple to prepare a revised list of works suitable for the Art Gallery and to make the necessary preparations, and this he did with his customary thoroughness. In February 1886 he submitted a detailed schedule of works to be removed from the various areas of Guildhall together with a plan of their arrangement in the Gallery, as well as a list of the remaining works which could be rearranged to fill the ensuing gaps. (One can only guess at Dicksee's feelings about this.) His Gallery plan included two rows of seats placed back to back, for which he suggested using the best of the benches from the Old Council Chamber. (Presumably these could not be made available, since in May the City Architect was instructed to provide benches 'at an Expence not exceeding £60, the seats to be of a Dark Crimson colour'; perhaps these were the ottomans supplied by the firm Cooper and Holt, who two years later complained their bill was still unpaid.) He informed the Committee that attendants would be required for security as soon as works began to enter the Gallery, suggesting that like the third class attendants in the Library ('men of excellent character'), they might receive 31/6 per week, with uniform. (William Cave and Charles Phillip Jones were appointed out of five candidates the following month, after the Committee had approved the hours and duties that Temple proposed for them.) Finally, he prompted them to instruct him to draw up a code of rules and regulations for the Gallery before its opening to the public. In March Temple reported that the City Architect had handed over to him the keys of the Gallery, and that works of art were now being removed to it; most of the principal works had been conveyed there when he next reported on April 12, including John Singleton Copley's enormous *Defeat of the Floating Batteries at Gibraltar, 1782* which had been taken down from the East wall of the Common Council Chamber where it had hung since 1815, rolled around a drum for removal to the Gallery and there restretched and reframed. For their part, the Committee had remembered to instruct Temple in February to provide information for the picture labels, which were to be of gilded

Sir Alfred Temple.

Guildhall Library, Prints and Maps Collection

wood and bear the artist's name and dates, title of picture, name of donor and date of presentation.

The Committee had high expectations that many donations of works of art would shortly be forthcoming. In December 1885 the Town Clerk had written to the Livery Companies to enquire if they would contribute any works of art or money for the purchase of works (a further letter requesting support and assistance was sent to 12 companies in 1888). Among the first contributions was a cheque for 100 guineas from the Vintners' Company, while the earliest presentations by individuals included *Flirtation* by Seymour Lucas (Henry Clarke) and *Scene from a Winter's Tale* by William Hamilton (Alderman Truscott). These and other gifts were acknowledged in the speech which Temple had written for the Chairman to deliver at the opening of the Gallery, at midday on June 24 1886:

'It has long been felt that this City, with its great wealth and position among the cities of the world, should possess a public Art Gallery, a fitting companion to the Schools of Education and Music now under the care of the Corporation and in which important institutions it takes so much interest. In the past year on the motion of Mr Henry Clarke, the Court of Common Council unanimously agreed to a Resolution, the effect of which has been the bringing together in one centre the Paintings and other works that now adorn these walls. These have been gathered mainly from the (hitherto somewhat scattered) possessions of the Corporation, but it is at the same time a most gratifying feature, that thus early in the day we have to gratefully acknowledge not only the liberality of Members of our own body who have made some notable presentations, but also the hearty and susbstantial encouragement of some of the great Livery Companies whose public spirited example we have every reason to hope will be ere long followed by others, so that in course of time, and, we trust, at no distant date, that which is at present what we may not inaptly term a nucleus collection may become a well filled Art Gallery, that shall prove a source, not merely of gratification but of profitable study, and useful instruction'.

Temple, in his memoirs, recorded that at a banquet held to celebrate the Gallery's opening, the President of the Royal Academy, Sir Frederic Leighton, described it as 'the commencement of an undertaking conceived on bold lines [...] which I venture to prophesy will have very far reaching effects'. However, established with no purchase budget or exhibition programme, the Gallery was, as Temple went on to note, 'quiescent [...] It did not demonstrate itself in any way as a factor of consequence in the art world.' Although there were 43,351 visitors to the Gallery in its first 12 months, the Library Committee must have been dismayed by the unfavourable comparison with the provinces made by the *Art Journal* in 1887 in its article 'The Guildhall and the City of London': 'Besides the library and

H E Tidmarsh (1854-1939): The Library Corridor adjoining Guildhall Art Gallery, c.1890.

watercolour; Guildhall Library, Prints and Maps Collection

the museum there is now a picture gallery connected with the Guildhall. [...] There are some interesting old city views and some fine portraits, but on the whole it is to be hoped that the same liberality which so greatly improved the library may soon be applied to the pictures. A small annual grant, properly administered, and the money spent, say, only at an annual exhibition of modern art in the city, would be a great boon to artists, and would soon lead to the formation of a worthy gallery. [...] What has been done by Liverpool, Manchester, Sheffield, and by the great Australian cities, entirely throws the modest little collection of London into the shade'.

In March 1887 the Committee agreed that it would be desirable to hold a small Loan Exhibition and went so far as to consider costs and plans for alterations to the old Bankruptcy Courts, but nothing further happened. It was Temple who in June 1888 drew their attention to the imminent move of the City of London Court from the 'spacious

Plans dated 12 August 1889
for the extension of the Art
Gallery into the central portion
of the building.

Corporation of London Records Office

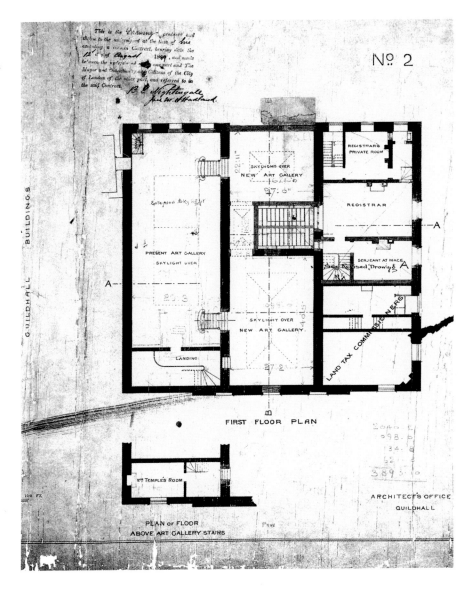

apartments adjacent to the Gallery' into a new building nearby. This offered a perfect opportunity to extend the Gallery's limited space, and the idea was discussed with the Law and City Courts Committee and the City Lands Committee during the rest of the year. In March 1889 the Library Committee approved the City Architect's plan for the new conversion as recommended by its Fine Art Sub Committee, with the additional requirement that the floors of both galleries should be made fireproof. (The City of London Society of

Artists' aims to establish an art academy were recalled in the same period, when discussions were held with the Charity Commission to see if funds arising from obsolete charities could be made available for the establishment of an Art School. Unfortunately the Commissioners were of the opinion that it did not 'sufficiently come within the statutory conditions requiring them to apply their funds for the benefits of the poorer classes'.) In July 1889, with work on the extension about to commence, Temple was instructed to remove all the pictures for storage in the Reading Room of the Library, which would have to be closed, and to hand over the building to the Architect on July 25. In October the Architect informed the Committee that the Gallery would not be ready until the end of the year, but in fact it was not until summer 1890 that the extended Gallery could be reopened with Temple's deferred Loan Exhibition of pictures.

The recommended alterations to the building included new parquet flooring 'as being uninjurious to the Pictures and more economical'; this was later amended to a carpet selected by the Chairman and two of the members, with an 18 inch margin all round of stained and varnished wood floor. A new entrance from the Library passage was made into the Gallery, designed so that the upper part of the framework could be removed to allow large paintings to pass through. In February 1890 the Committee accepted the City Architect's recommended wallpaper for the Gallery, cost 4s 6d per roll. (The colour was not recorded in the Committee's papers but Temple noted in his memoirs that the walls of the exhibition were red.) But even at this late stage the Committee was still considering amended plans, and on February 20 1890 approved a new 'Plan A [...] for fitting up and adapting the interior of the Gallery, and to include proper accommodation for the Secretary and his staff' at an estimated cost of £600. Meanwhile the Committee had also been considering the exhibition arrangements, and Temple had submitted a list of 'Old and Modern Paintings', together with an estimate of probable expenses. It was resolved that the exhibition should run between June and August, and in March Temple submitted a final list of works with the names of the owners, to whom the Town Clerk was instructed to write.

It was the success of Temple's fifteen ambitious Loan Exhibitions that put the Gallery truly on the map. The newly enlarged Gallery in 1890 now offered 412 linear feet of hanging space instead of 190, and the inaugural exhibition of Flemish, Dutch and British Pictures was opened on June 10 by the Lord Mayor (no refreshments were served but a string band was engaged to play on that and the following day, which were a private view with admission by ticket only). By the time the exhibition closed on August 31 it had been seen by 109,383 visitors, and on the last afternoon the crowd waiting to get in was so large that it filled Guildhall Yard, and entry had to be regulated so that as 50 exited another

The Art Gallery extension
with pictures from the
William Dunnett Bequest
and others, c.1890-1897.

*Guildhall Library, Prints and
Maps Collection*

50 were admitted. (Perhaps it was because of wear and tear caused by all the visitors that in
November the treadway of the Art Gallery carpet was covered with Kamptulikon, a form of
floorcloth.) Gratified by the success of the exhibition, the Committee granted Temple a
month's leave after its close, and backdated his salary increase.

Despite the success of their first effort, when the idea of holding further exhibitions
was raised by Henry Clarke in 1891 the Library Committee turned it down. However, it
had some supporters among Committee members, notably William Rome, an expert col-
lector of antiquities and a Past Master of the Painter Stainers Company. It was eventually
resolved to hold a second exhibition in 1892, which attracted more than twice as many
visitors as the first. During the third exhibition in 1894 the Gallery opened for the first time

on a Sunday, and Temple described how 'Guildhall Yard and the adjacent streets presented an unusual spectacle; people crowding in, the patient queue reaching to Basinghall Street round to Gresham Street, and almost to the Bank of England. It was the prelude to all the museums and galleries being opened to the public on Sunday afternoons'. In 1897 – the year of the Queen's Diamond Jubilee – the Committee must have been pleased at the laudatory remarks of the *Art Journal* for the current exhibition ('Loan Collection of Pictures by Painters who have flourished during Her Majesty's Reign'): 'The City Fathers are singularly fortunate in their Art Director. In face of the strong rivalry in London of the collections at Earl's Court and of the Crystal Palace, and of the Brussels, Copenhagen and Venice exhibitions on the Continent, Mr A G Temple has brought together a superb gathering of the best of the Victorian era paintings. The pre-Raphaelites are particularly fine, and generally

Signing the Visitors Book in Guildhall Art Gallery, unknown artist, after 1893 (?).
Guildhall Library, Prints and Maps Collection

Gallery 1 in 1917. Copley's *Defeat of the Floating Batteries* was taken down in case of air raids in 1915 and not rehung until 1922.

Guildhall Library, Prints and Maps Collection

this free exhibition under the auspices of the Lord Mayor and his Council reflects the greatest credit on the Director and the Art Committee. The public show their appreciation by entering literally in crowds all the time, and doubtless during the Jubilee fetes the Gallery will meet with great attention from visitors to London'. The exhibition of Spanish pictures of 1901 was so popular that it was extended for four weeks beyond its original three months; 3,000 visitors per day were recorded and a Spanish edition of the catalogue was published. Opening the following year's exhibition of eighteenth-century French and English pictures, the Lord Mayor said that Temple 'had the entire confidence of the Corporation and but for his tact and artistic judgement the exhibition could hardly have been got together'. In 1905 (a year in which no exhibition was held), the *Morning Advertiser* described the series as 'one of the few really good things, from the artistic point of view, of which London in recent years has been able to boast, one of the few things indeed that kept Cockneydom from hanging its head in shame before the artistic enthusiasms of such provincial towns as Manchester, Leeds and Liverpool. One can, in fact, hardly calculate the amount of good which these exhibitions at the Guildhall have done. [...] Starting out to educate the clerk, the Corporation have found themselves the promoters of one of the most successful and widely and deservedly popular shows in the country'. However, the cost of mounting the exhibitions was becoming increasingly expensive. With William Rome's death in October 1907 an important advocate of the exhibitions was lost, and the Committee resolved to discontinue

Guildhall Art Gallery, 1912

Guildhall Library, Prints and Maps Collection

them. They had been seen by a total of 2,734,561 visitors and, as the *Morning Advertiser* had expressed it in 1905, the Corporation had 'created a welcome taste for art in an enormous public which they [had] now determined to starve'.

Temple's bitterness about the Committee's decision was only obliquely expressed in his book *Guildhall Memories* (1918), but it could not have been helped by the fact that having earlier been involved in an unsuccessful scheme to induce Henry Tate to build his National Gallery of British Art on a City site, in 1897 he had turned down the opportunity to be the new Tate Gallery's first Keeper because the Treasury would not allow him also to retain his existing appointment at Guildhall. Temple had thought 'that the duties attaching to the position at the Tate Gallery would not occupy my entire time once the pictures were arranged on the walls [...] I was not a little actuated by the scope for action which the Guildhall Art Gallery presented when placed beside the appointment in question, in which I could discern only a very limited field for activity.' After the cessation of his Guildhall exhibitions Temple remained in the Corporation's service but transferred his energies to the organising of prestigious shows elsewhere in Britain and on the Continent, for which he became much decorated and greatly honoured. As well as arranging the Guildhall exhibitions he had always taken every opportunity to promote the Gallery in other ways and to

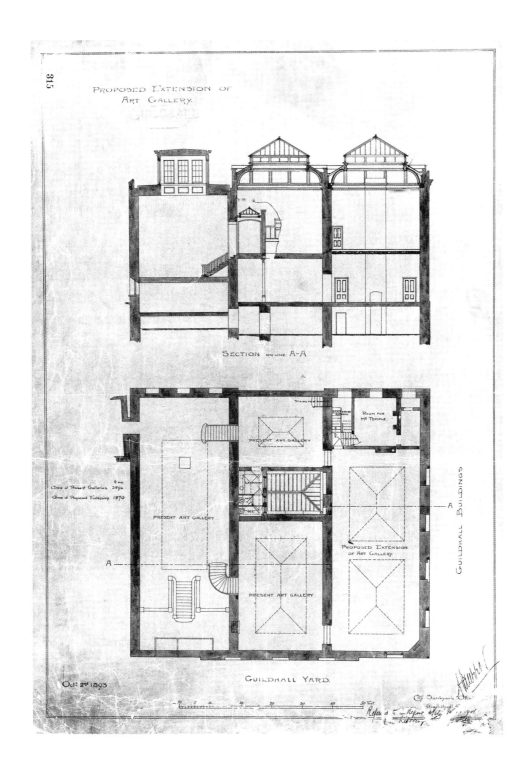

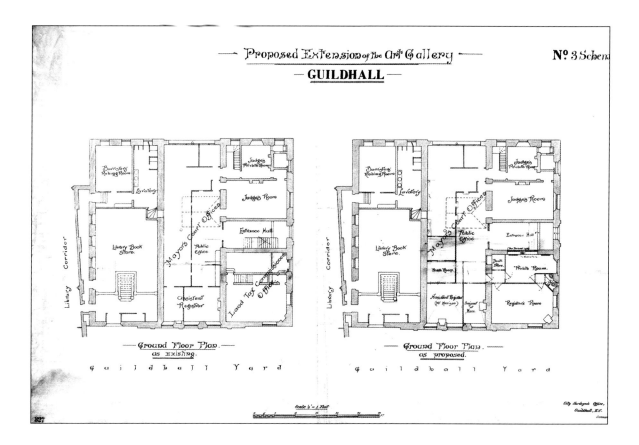

Proposed Extension of the Art Gallery, Ground Floor Plan, dated 4 October 1897.

Corporation of London Record Office

attract donations and bequests of works of art. It was due to Temple's persuasion that in 1902 Charles Gassiot bequeathed his collection of 127 Victorian paintings, including works by Tissot and Millais, while in 1911 he bought W S Burton's *Wounded Cavalier* for the Gallery at his own expense (and without Committee approval), being eventually reimbursed some months later with money solicited from various members. In 1921 he persuaded Lady Millais to part with *The Woodman's Daughter* for £1,500 (£600 less than she had originally wanted), and Lord Bearsted to provide the money for it; four years later he got Bearsted to buy Lord Leighton's *The Music Lesson* for the Gallery, and gave the Library Committee a strong hint that the existing purchase budget of £500 was far too low for the purchase of major works.

Despite attempts in the 1880s and 1890s to define the relative positions of the Secretary and the Curator, these had become no clearer. The Library Committee had wavered between expressing antipathy to Dicksee's unsolicited advice about the Art Gallery and attempting to add responsibility for the paintings therein to his existing duties (it was not clear where this would have left Temple). For its part, the City Lands Committee remained supportive of its officer, sending Dicksee rather than Temple to Vicopelago in Italy in 1889 to pack up and send back the paintings, sculptures and other items bequeathed to the Corporation the previous year by retired City businessman William Dunnett. (Once the bequest was received and put on display in the Old Council Chamber, the Library Committee nonetheless succeeded in appropriating it for the Gallery.) Dicksee retired in 1896, and Temple took over his duties in an honorary capacity, carrying out the dual roles of Director (as he had become by this time) of the Art Gallery and Curator of Works of Art. He officially retired in October1913, but continued to discharge the duties of the two posts at an annual honorarium of 100 guineas per annum, reporting to both the Library Committee and to the City Lands Committee. In March 1920 the latter reported to the

Proposed Extension of the Art Gallery, First Floor Plan, dated 4 October 1897. The room in the upper right corner is faintly inscribed in pencil 'Mr Temple'. Further inscriptions state: 'Hanging space about 4660 ft' and 'LAID BEFORE SUB & GRAND LIBRARY COMMITTEE 4th OCTR. 1897. COST STATED TO BE ABOUT £1600 WHICH IS TO INCLUDE FIREPROOF FLOOR.' and 'Laid before City Lands by Library Com. 13.X.97'.

Corporation of London Record Office

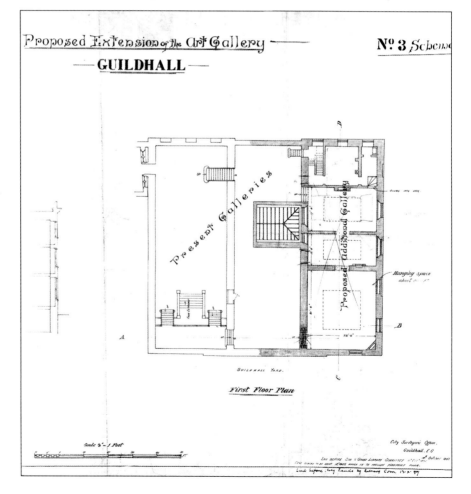

Court of Common Council that their attention had been drawn to the anomaly of the two posts and the reporting procedure. The Court agreed that the offices should be merged into a single position under the control of the Library Committee, allowing the Director of the Art Gallery to be responsible for all works belonging to the Corporation, regardless of where they were housed. Sir Alfred Temple (as he had become) died in 1928 after an illness during which the Librarian, J L Douthwaite, had been made Acting Director. On recommending that Douthwaite be confirmed as Director of the Art Gallery in addition to his office as Librarian, the Library Committee noted in their report that 'at some future time, no doubt [we] will have to submit to your Honourable Court recommendations of a more lasting character when the permanent Art Gallery, at present in contemplation, is built, and when the existing arrangements may have to be reviewed'.

Alterations to the Gallery's accommodation and an extension into the southern portion of the block were made during the 1890s, while a major rebuilding scheme that included both the Gallery and the buildings on the opposite side of Guildhall Yard was dropped because of the first War. Despite the addition in 1922 of rooms formerly occupied by the Income Tax Commissioners pressure on Gallery space had become acute, and on November 2 1925 the Library Committee reported on the problem to Court. Out of a collection of 1040 works, only 404 were in the Art Gallery, the remaining 636 being either scattered about the Guildhall, the Mansion House and other Corporation buildings, or in store. They concluded: 'The present conditions all point to the need for a more commodious

Plan of the Guildhall, showing the extent of the Gallery in 1912 and its relation to the Library, Portland House and other neighbouring buildings. Signed by the City Surveyor Sydney Perks FRIBA, FSA and dated January 1912.

Corporation of London Record Office

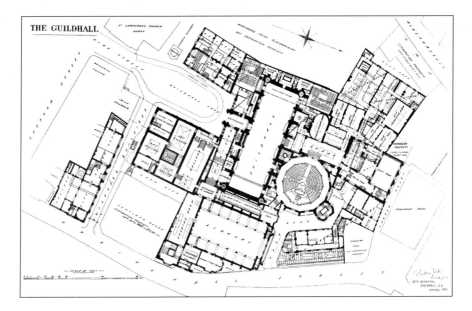

RIGHT: Proposed new Art Gallery in the East Block of the Guildhall Improvement Scheme, by Sydney Perks FSA, City Architect, c.1911.

Corporation of London Record Office

BELOW: The Guildhall Rebuilding Scheme (Ground Floor), by Sir Giles Gilbert Scott, dated January 1936, and showing a larger Art Gallery expanded to include the Portland House site to the East.

Corporation of London Record Office

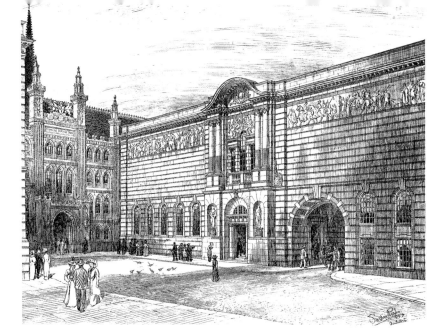

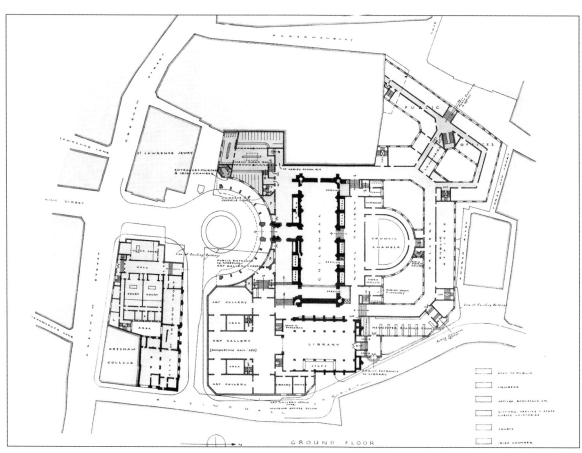

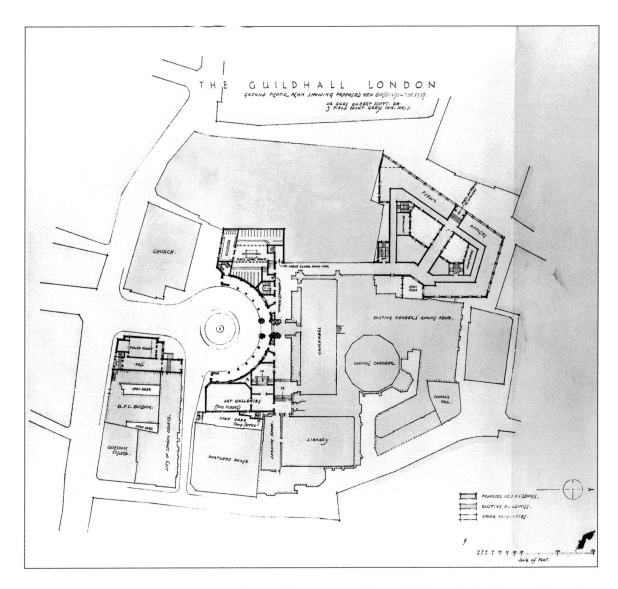

The Guildhall Rebuilding
Scheme (Ground Floor), by
Sir Giles Gilbert Scott, dated
November 1937, very much
reduced in extent from the
previous version.

Corporation of London Record Office

Gallery, in which the different sections of Art could be kept distinct. We are of the opinion
that the time has now arrived when a new Fine Art Gallery should be erected and recom-
mend that we should be authorised to consider and report to your Honourable Court our
proposal in the matter and upon the whole subject of art within the City'. Although their
report was referred to the Finance Committee in connection with plans for rebuilding the
Guildhall complex, nothing came of it. A further Guildhall rebuilding scheme designed
in 1935 by Sir Giles Gilbert Scott RA proposed inter alia a larger new Art Gallery that

included the Portland House site to the East, while a modified version of the scheme in 1937 showed a somewhat smaller Gallery. Neither scheme came to fruition, and in 1939 the outbreak of War changed the situation entirely.

By 1939 the Gallery comprised offices on its top floor, while beneath was the large Gallery I from which three further galleries led off at the south east corner. At the north east corner of Gallery I was an exit to the loggia or landing outside the Library, and in the basement were storerooms. The original crimson carpet had been replaced by polished parquet with painted black skirting boards, while the walls were hung with a dark red silky fabric. Big pictures too large to be accommodated elsewhere were hung in Gallery I, arranged evenly and close together but not hung according to school, date or theme. The other galleries contained smaller works, one being devoted to the collection of London watercolours by Alistair Macdonald after its presentation by Lord Wakefield in 1936. But the Gallery was completely full, and only 450 works were on display out of a total in 1939 of 1,100, while 300 were in store and 350 were hung in other Corporation departments. The lack of any other VIP reception rooms at Guildhall meant that during state visits or on other important functions the Gallery had to be closed for several days beforehand while it was decorated with luxurious carpets, antique furniture, potted palms and, on occasion, even a royal cloakroom festooned in white bunting. The Gallery was always closed between November 6 and 12 in connection with Lord Mayor's Day, and the Library too had often to be closed for receptions, so that the Committee and staff came to bitterly regret the disruption in public service that these events entailed.

During the First World War some measures had been taken to protect works of art in case of air raids, but it was evident that when the second War came more complex arrangements would be necessary and after the Munich crisis in September 1938 the Library Committee laid plans for the removal of the more valuable property in its care. The Museum was closed to the public from February 1939 and, while some objects were too large to move or too firmly fixed in place, most of its holdings were taken to Upper Westwood Quarry, Wiltshire, which had been prepared by the Office of Works as a store and housed material from the British Museum, National Gallery and Victoria and Albert Museum. In May certain works of art were evacuated to free storage at Newbury, Berkshire; Bruton, Somerset (Hugh Sexey's Hospital); Trowbridge Town Hall, Wiltshire; and Maidenhatch, a building provided free of charge by Tate & Lyle at Tidmarsh village near Pangbourne, Berkshire. Additional accommodation was rented from Bourlet & Sons at Wicken Park near Fenny Stratford, Northamptonshire and from Sir Charles Russell at Swallowfield Park, Berkshire, at £125 per annum plus the cost of coal for winter heating and 10s per week

OVERLEAF P.30, TOP:
The Coronation Luncheon at Guildhall, 1937 by Frank Salisbury was presented by Lord Wakefield to the Corporation of London in 1939. This photograph shows the artist speaking in front of it at the unveiling ceremony on March 16. The picture is shown in the most prominent position in the Gallery, until recently occupied by Copley's *Defeat of the Floating Batteries*. Above it has been hung Opie's *Murder of Rizzio* (1787), while on either side are some of the series of 22 Fire Judges by John Michael Wright (1670s), with *Oxwich Bay* (1851) by Clarkson Stanfield beneath on the right and *Commerce and Sea Power* (1898) by W L Wyllie on the left.
Guildhall Library, Prints and Maps Collection

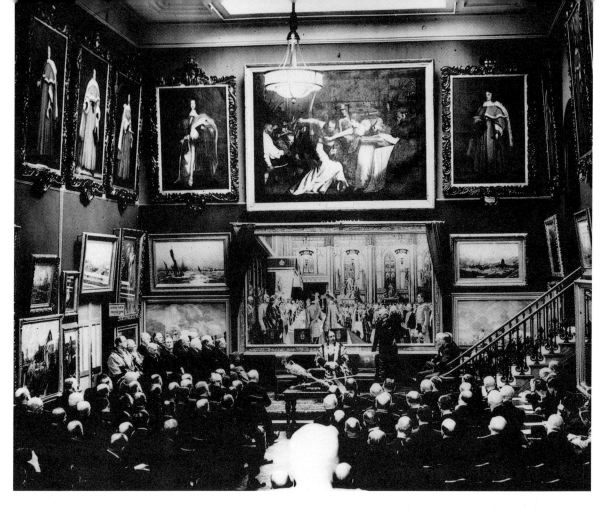

Packing up works of art, 1939.

*Guildhall Library, Prints and
Maps Collection*

for two maids to see to the fires. In some cases pictures went to one store while their frames and glass went to another. When a state of emergency was declared on August 24 some Guildhall Library material was removed to safety but most of the printed books were left in situ, as it was felt that the Library could not flourish outside London and that its continued service to the public justified the risk involved.

At their meeting on November 8 1939 the Committee learnt from the Director that more pictures had left for the country the previous month. He continued: 'Apart from a few decorative pictures at Mansion House, some comparatively modern portraits in the Committee Rooms the large canvases in the Council Chamber Lobby, and miscellaneous material in the store which I do not think is worth moving, there is nothing left except the series of Fire Judges, a painting by Opie [*The Murder of Rizzio*, presented by Alderman Boydell c.1793] and Copley's canvas of the defeat of the Spanish floating batteries at Gibraltar [...]. The painting by Opie is of no particular significance as far as your Committee's Gallery is concerned [!], and my object in keeping it here is in the hope that a little later on I may be permitted to experiment with its restoration. The Fire Judges cannot well be removed from the Gallery; their frames are almost as interesting as the paintings, and I am hoping that Mr Surveyor will be able to provide a measure of safety for them in a room under Gallery no.1.'

Over the next few months discussions ensued about whether it was better to protect Copley's *Defeat* from 'concussion' by boarding it up where it hung with timber (cost: £31.3s.6d and a special licence for the wood required from the Ministry of Supply), or with wood and 'metal-faced ply-board' (cost: £54 and the materials hard to obtain), or whether it should be rolled and stored in the Crypt beneath Guildhall as it had been in 1915. The need to make a decision became acute when in the terrible air raid of Sunday December 29 1940 the roof of the Guildhall, the Common Council Chamber and the Aldermen's Court Room were all destroyed by fire. The Library roof was also damaged, and 25,000 printed books were burnt while many thousands more were damaged by water. Several print collections and the prints catalogue stored in the Library Bridge were also lost. Small in comparison was the number of works lost from the art collection – approximately 98, many of them marble busts located in the Council Chamber, and its Lobby and Corridor, together with 43 marble pedestals and 7 frames. The 22 portraits of Fire Judges by John Michael Wright had been placed in the Crypt and were soused by the water being used to put out the conflagration above. It was decided to evacuate the Department's remaining holdings, and on April 8 1941, having been taken down earlier, unstretched, its surface protected, rolled and crated, Copley's *Defeat* was taken to Swallowfield – only a month before Guildhall Art Gallery itself was destroyed.

The air raid of Saturday May 10 1941 took place during a full moon and was even worse than December's. Big Ben, the Houses of Parliament and Westminster Hall were seriously damaged by high explosive and incendiaries, and among the City's terrible losses Guildhall Art Gallery burnt down with the loss of more than 250 works. The raid coincided with a low water level in the Thames, while it was also probable that mains had been damaged in previous raids, and all over the City there were desperate calls for water to extinguish the fires. John Bromley, then a Principal Assistant in the Library, afterwards wrote an account that vividly conveys the bravery and persistence of those on duty that night:

'I was awakened a few minutes after midnight and told to report at once for duty. As I came into the Library sparks and pieces of incendiary bomb were falling from roof to floor. [...] As I extinguished the pieces of bomb on the floor I could hear activity from watchers overhead. On my way to the roof I stopped in the Porch to telephone to Headquarters and report the fire. On reaching the roof I found members of the squad connecting the hose to the hydrant. We laid the hose to the fire, but found, upon turning on the supply, that the pressure was insufficient to carry over the parapet. A stirrup-pump party was working on the fire which appeared to have caught the timbers exposed by the previous fire. The fire brigade was then informed, and I returned to the Library and with the others connected the hose at the hydrant by the Library Bridge, but again the pressure was too weak to be of use.

'The Library fire was caused by one of a number of incendiary bombs that had fallen on and in Guildhall. Another had also ignited in the Mess Room at the top of the Art Gallery and was attended to by the squad. [...] Within about half an hour the fire brigade arrived and dealt with the Library and Art Gallery fires and eventually appeared to have put them out. Shortly after, however, the fire in the roof broke out again and the fire brigade, being still on the premises, started to deal with the flames, but almost before the water reached the roof the supply failed. It was then discovered that the Art Gallery was once more alight. [...] I telephoned the ARP Controller and said that the fire, if not immediately dealt with, was a threat to the Library and the office of the MOH [Medical Officer of Health]. The Controller said he would do what he could, but similar reports of lack of water were reaching him from all over the City. [...] The fire had by now reached the bottom of the staircase outside the Director's room, and I went in and rescued some portable property. From this time until it became obvious that such a method was useless, the members of the fire squad including the Hallkeeper's staff used stirrup-pumps upon the fire.

'I telephoned to Control again [...] suggesting that if the dam in the Yard could be filled, much might be done to save the premises. I also [...] found the officer in charge of the fire brigade outside the Public Health Department entrance, attempting, with a number

Gallery I in January 1941: drying out books from Guildhall Library which were damaged by water during the air raid of December 29 1940. All the pictures have been removed from the walls except Opie's *Murder of Rizzio* and Salisbury's *Coronation Luncheon at Guildhall*, whose glass has been taped in case of blast.

Guildhall Library, Prints and Maps Collection

of men and very little water, to subdue a fire in a building opposite. We appealed to him to fill the dam. I suggested with deference to his experience, that the Gallery might yet be in part saved if that were done. He was sceptical about the result of such a measure, slightly resentful at my interference, and adamant about the impractibility of filling the dam. There were, in his opinion, no means for doing this and even if it were done the water made available would have little effect upon the fire since it would be exhausted in a minute or two. He eventually agreed to come to see the fire in order to give us an opinion as to its probable development [...]. The officer did not think there was any immediate threat and thought that the water would be through soon.

'During the time that our efforts were engaged upon the major fire, a constant patrol had to be kept upon the Library, for sparks from a fire in Basinghall Street were being blown onto the roof; small fires began also upon the Public Health Department and Irish Chamber roofs.

'My last telephone call to the Control room elicited the fact that the Controller had been in touch with Regional Headquarters and had passed on at once the suggestion to fill the dam. [...] It was now daylight, and with the aid of three wardens we managed to move out into the Yard the crated busts and their pedestals which were inside the Art Gallery entrance. Farley and Cox [the attendants] arrived soon after the 'All Clear' and Farley closed the iron door from the Art Gallery into the Library Corridor. The Town Clerk arrived about this time and I pointed out to him that the dam was just then being filled from portable tanks that were being brought in in relays. [...] After several attempts from about 5.30 a.m., I succeeded in speaking to the Librarian on the telephone; he was able to reach here to take charge about 9.45 a.m.'

The two crated busts were in fact the life-size sculpture of Henry Irving as Hamlet by Edward Onslow Ford and G F Watt's *Clytie* with its square marble plinth, packed up ready for removal to the country. 'These would have been unquestionably destroyed', reported the Librarian to Committee in June, 'but for the energy of Mr J F Bromley [...] who, while the fire was raging, obtained sufficient labour to move these very heavy cases out of harm's way.'

Most of the works lost from the Gallery had been in its basement store. They included 164 oil paintings, drawings, watercolours and prints, and 20 marble, bronze and plaster sculptures together with assorted marble and wooden pedestals. Fifty-seven uncatalogued items included sundry frames and 8 paintings 'found in the Gallery on the death of the late Director'. Some paintings survived even though their frames and glass were burnt, while a number of busts escaped despite the loss of their columns. It took some time to complete the task of digging pictures and busts from the rubble and identifying them, and some items were simply never found.

It is difficult to reconcile the different lists of those lost and damaged in the raids of 1940 and 1941, since some works assessed at the time as merely damaged were in fact so badly affected by fire and water that they were later written off, while others listed as destroyed survived in store to be restored years later. Further, among the losses in 1941 were items of art deposited by other owners, uncatalogued pictures, frames and miscellaneous items. Works of art had been included in the Corporation's general insurance policy, under which the maximum claim was £5,000. The claim submitted in respect of works lost or damaged on December 29 1940 was £7,075. In October 1945 the War Damage Commission made a settlement of £4,925, which represented the maximum claim allowable less a premium of £75. A further claim of £3,351.10s was agreed in respect of the losses of May 10 1941, making the total sum recovered against the loss of more than 300 works of art £8,276.10s plus interest at 2½%.

The Gallery's destruction offered an opportunity to correct both the temporary and makeshift nature of its accommodation and the lack of any clear acquisition policy. Reporting to the Library Committee on October 18 1943, the Chairman pointed out that 'the situation in London is entirely different from that of any provincial city. In London we have the National Gallery, the National Portrait Gallery, the Tate Gallery, the Victoria and Albert Museum, etc., with none of which can the Corporation hope to compete. [...] On the other hand the Corporation has already the nucleus of what might become a first class

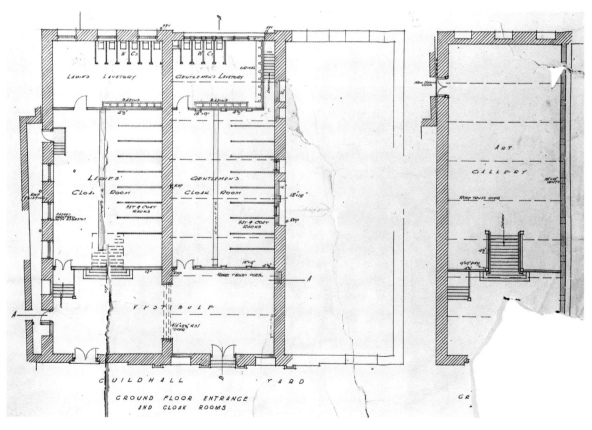

specialised collection which would attract visitors from all over the world.' A further memorandum approved on November 24 1944 specified that in future acquisitions should consist principally of works of London interest, and of other works of outstanding merit.

Any permanent building for the Corporation's collection of works of art could only be considered in the context of the restoration of the whole Guildhall site. However, it was felt essential to provide space for receptions, and a 'temporary' structure was hastily begun on the cleared site behind the old Gallery's ground floor facade – all that now remained of it. This new structure roughly followed the plan of the old Gallery I, with cloakrooms beneath, and occupied only about half of the old site. Although its principal purpose was ceremonial, the Librarian and Director reminded his Committee in April 1946 that 'an ancillary purpose of the new apartment is the display of works of art'.

Until now the Art Gallery's holdings had still been in store around the country. 98 oils and watercolours were at Bruton, Somerset, while 115 pictures, 22 sculptures and 12 frames were at Newbury. 15 paintings were held at the Upper Westwood Quarry. The 22 Fire Judge portraits had ended up at Wicken Park after their soaking, while 146 oils, 321 watercolour, 7 sculptures and 27 frames, plus the Library's print collection and objects from the Guildhall Museum, were stored in the stables, the 'yellow drawing room' and the library at Swallowfield. An inspection of these repositories and of the Library and Museum collections was undertaken in 1945, and in September the Director reported on the problems of reassembling 100,000 books, 30,000 manuscripts, the works of art and all the Museum objects, together with the plate and other material on deposit from City churches and livery companies that had also been stored. A month later he reported that at Bruton the floor was damp and the packing of pictures had been affected. At Trowbridge a box containing manuscripts had rotted (though not its contents). As a result, the objects in both locations were returned to Guildhall, while the Committee instructed him to concentrate all other pictures at Swallowfield. (Extra rent had to be paid to the owner, who also asked to be reimbursed the £9.14s.9d he had had to spend on repairing the stable roof.) Pictures and other material were transferred to Swallowfield throughout 1946 and works were also returned to Guildhall. However, the space available for the Department's holdings was considerably less than it had been before the War. The Library still had its old reading and reference rooms, but in lieu of storerooms destroyed or unfit for use its basement – which had formerly housed the Guildhall Museum – was taken over for book storage; a further 20,000 volumes were stored in the basement of the Lord Mayor's and City of London Court. Thus deprived of its old accommodation, the Museum now occupied the Bridge, formerly a Library store, which offered less than an eighth of its original floor space.

The rebuilt Guildhall Art Gallery, date of photo unknown. In receding order, the paintings shown are *The Garden of Eden* (1901) by H G Riviere, Tissot's *Too Early* (1873) and *Clytemnestra* (1882) by the Hon. John Collier.
Guildhall Library, Prints and Maps Collection

Paintings were first hung in the new VIP reception room which had been built on the old Gallery site for a reception on July 19 1946, and the display was subsequently opened to the public. However, the building was not very suited to the purpose, being a hastily erected barn-like structure with a roof comprised of straw and asphalt blocks, unseasoned and unplaned wooden beams and thin steel girders, and a linoleum-covered floor of unseasoned timber planks which shrank to leave large gaps and eventually developed dry rot. The walls were painted a neutral pale grey or off-white, and pictures were hung in a single line on battens running along them at eye level. It was a far cry from the old Gallery's comparatively opulent interior, even when the floor was later covered with a richly patterned carpet similar to that used in ceremonial areas elsewhere at Guildhall. There were no offices, stores or workshop, and only 250 linear feet of hanging space. However, the 1950s and 1960s saw the development of a busy exhibitions programme in even this limited accommodation. A selection from the art collection was shown periodically for about a month at a time, as well as one from the Prints and Maps collection. Increasing numbers of art societies held their annual exhibitions in the Gallery, while the Children's Royal Academy, organised by the Royal Drawing Society, had been an annual feature since 1916. The Corporation sponsored two exhibitions – the Lord Mayor's Art Award, which exhibited the work of professional London artists, and the City of London Art Exhibition, which showed citizens' work. Between 1952 and 1972 the Keeper of Prints and Pictures, J L Howgego, organised a series of influential exhibitions that recalled Temple's efforts so many years before. Pressure on the limited and unsatisfactory storage spaces around Guildhall meant that increasing numbers of pictures had to be lent out, not only to Corporation officers and to the Mansion House and Old Bailey but also to schools, Livery Companies, the Palace of Westminster and further afield, to the Royal Military College of Science, Shrivenham and the Royal Naval College, Haslar, among many other locations. These opportunities offered the benefit of (semi) public display, together with the occasional drawbacks of theft, vandalism, neglect and the difficulty of achieving regular inspections of so many works in different locations.

In October 1949 the Director had reported on the past and present situation of the Department's holdings and on the needs of the future, reminding Members that 'Objects from the Museum are shown in a makeshift fashion in such odd spaces as are available [...] but this is regarded as a temporary measure pending the rebuilding of Guildhall, and the erection of a new Museum worthy of the Corporation and its extremely valuable collection.' Pointing out that there were currently no cloakrooms or lavatories for Library readers and visitors ('a situation without parallel in any other public institution'), he went on to detail the modest requirements of a rebuilt Art Gallery: '*1*. Main galleries (preferably in 3 or 4

Admiral of the Fleet Lord
Fraser of North Cape speaking
at the opening of the Third
Annual Exhibition of the
Society of Marine Artists
in Guildhall Art Gallery,
November 1948.

*Guildhall Library, Prints and
Maps Collection*

compartments) with a total hanging space of about 700 ft linear and top lighting. *2.* Print
Room, about 40' x 40', for the housing of the print collection, and accommodation of staff,
display of prints, etc. *3.* Work room for technical assistant. *4.* cloakroom and lavatory accommodation for Art Gallery staff. *5.* Storage rooms, two, 50' x 50' x 15' for large pictures.
Storage rooms, two, 30' x 30' x 10' for smaller pictures. *6.* Workshop with bench, 15' x 20' x 20'.'

It was not until 1954 that the special Guildhall Reconstruction Committee was set up
to deal with the enormous amount of restoration and rebuilding necessary, and in February
1955 the Library Committee submitted a resolution outlining their requirements for the
Library, Art Gallery and Museum, and requesting a meeting with the Architect commis-

sioned by the Corporation to undertake the restoration and new building, Sir Giles Gilbert Scott. Following the restoration of the Great Hall and the building of the North Block on the site of the destroyed Council Chamber, detailed discussions between the architects, the Guildhall Reconstruction Committee and the Library Committee ensued over the next few years. In 1960 it was decided that rather than build a new Council Chamber it would be better to employ the Library for Court meetings, and to build a new Library on the west side. (The Court of Common Council now meets in the Great Hall, and the Old Library is reserved for reception purposes.) The scheme allowed for a new 'dual purpose Art Gallery and Reception area for distinguished guests with Retiring Rooms etc adjoining'. It provided about 165 feet more hanging space than the pre-War Gallery, but the apparent gain was offset, the Director claimed, by the fact that whereas formerly pictures were double banked, the modern practice was to hang them in a single line with plenty of space between each. Furthermore, the plans incorporated a small gallery for exhibits from the print collection, 'a much needed accommodation which was not provided in the old Gallery'. The Committee realised that the proposals would allow the display of the permanent collection only, and that there would be no room for the exhibiting art societies – despite the fact that the Gallery was now such a popular venue that it had to turn away applicants. (It was agreed that the solution would be to transfer the temporary and largely amateur exhibitions to the proposed art gallery to be included in the new Barbican development on the bomb-ravaged neighbourhood around St Giles Cripplegate. This idea had evaporated by the time Barbican Art Gallery finally opened in 1982 with the brief to house major exhibitions of international significance.) No provision was made in the scheme for the Guildhall Museum, which had been lodged in the Royal Exchange since 1955. It had since become a well known attraction and in 1959 had received 125,000 visitors. A working party had been set up to draft a constitution for a proposed Museum of London to be formed from the amalgamation of the Guildhall Museum and the London Museum, and this was achieved in 1975 when the objects formerly at Guildhall were formally transferred to the new entity.

The rebuilding of Guildhall Art Gallery on its old site was eventually scheduled for completion in 1976 as part of Phase V of the Guildhall Reconstruction Scheme. It was envisaged that the existing structure would be handed over to contractors for demolition in 1973 but in June that year all work on Phase V was frozen. Twelve months later the Chairman of the Policy Committee informed the Reconstruction Committee that the current financial situation permitted only a holding operation to be effected. This would allow completion of the new Guildhall Library and West Wing but not the rebuilding of the Art Gallery. When the Reconstruction Committee learnt in February 1975 that expenditure

ILDHALL PRECINCTS RECONSTRUCTION · PHASE V · SKETCH SHOWING PROPOSED ART GALLERY AT EAST SIDE OF THE YARD · ARCHITECTS' SIR GILES SCOTT, SON & PARTNER. 1972

Guildhall Precincts
Reconstruction, Phase V, by
Sir Giles Scott, Son & Partner,
1972. At the left of the sketch
is the new Aldermen's Court
Room. Adjoining the Guildhall
Porch is the Ambulatory, with
the proposed new Art Gallery
shown at the far side of
Guildhall Yard.

*Guildhall Library, Prints and
Maps Collection*

on Phase V could not be provided in the coming financial year, it was forced to resolve to defer the rest of the scheme indefinitely.

For a decade more the 'temporary' Gallery continued to house a full programme of exhibitions mounted by various art societies and other bodies, although internal exhibitions had long ceased. Certain measures were taken in the 1970s to improve security after the National Security Advisor had written to the Town Clerk stating that this element was very poor. Eventually, in December 1985 the Corporation decided that the 'temporary' Gallery and the vacant rubble-strewn lot behind it, had been an eyesore for long enough, and the pressing need for improved VIP reception accommodation and more office space resulted in the decision finally to build on the old Art Gallery site. A feasibility report was prepared which incorporated details of the new Art Gallery requirements provided by the Director of Libraries and Art Galleries, and an architect was appointed – Richard Gilbert Scott, the son of Sir Giles, who had assisted his father in the earlier Guildhall restoration and reconstruction and had designed the new Guildhall Library and West Wing of 1974.

The 'temporary' Gallery was demolished in 1987, followed by the demolition of Portland House behind it and fronting Basinghall Street. Before any construction work began the Museum of London Archaeological Service carried out an investigation in the course of which they discovered not only the expected mediaeval remains but also Saxon remains and those of the Roman Amphitheatre whose existence had been suspected but whose location was unknown. The site was accordingly scheduled, and a considerable amount of work was required to re-design the building around these discoveries, which remain extant at basement level while the building itself extends for two further floors below them.

The Art Gallery occupies three floors of the new building (two being public display while the third comprises picture stores and conservation studio and workshop areas); further galleries connecting to the new structure have been made from the vaulted Victorian basements beneath the Old Print Room. A major element of the building is a wall rising the height of two floors for the display of John Singleton Copley's *Defeat of the Floating Batteries at Gibraltar, 1782.* This picture had remained rolled up in store for more than 40 years after it was taken down in 1941 and sent away to safety, because no wall large enough to display it had been found either within the Corporation or elsewhere. After

The original Gallery facade and post war structure shortly before demolition in 1987.
Reproduced by courtesy of Jeremy Johnson.

ABOVE: The new Guildhall
Art Gallery, March 1999.

RIGHT: Bringing John
Singleton Copley's *Defeat of
the Floating Batteries* into the
Gallery on February 25 1999.

Main picture: Séamus Mckenna
Other pictures: Jeremy Johnson

TOP AND CENTRE:
Michele Tedesco's *A Pythagorea School Invaded by Sybarites* is brought into the Gallery on January 27 1999.

RIGHT: Edward Armitage's *Herods Birthday Feast* arrives in the Gallery on January 27 1999.

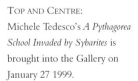

remedial work was carried out on its rat-nibbled edges and numerous tears by the conservators of the Area Museums Service for South East England, in 1985 the staff of the Historic Buildings and Monuments Commission (now English Heritage) Conservation Studio spent several years on the conservation of the enormous canvas. Conservation of its original eighteenth-century frame in 1996 included cleaning, replacing the lost moulding, gilding and carving matching sections to enlarge the frame to its original dimensions (it had probably been cut down in 1886 when it was first moved to the Art Gallery from the Old Council Chamber). The filling, retouching and varnishing of the canvas was carried out under the supervision of Gallery staff once the painting was in situ, thus providing the first opportunity in more than half a century to see this exciting picture. Surrounding Copley's painting are pictures presented by Alderman John Boydell in the 1790s, while other parts of the Gallery display London subjects, Victorian paintings and sculpture and modern works. The main gallery, which also fulfills the function of a reception area for distinguished guests, displays royal and civic portraits and ceremonial subjects.

After Guildhall Art Gallery was destroyed in the Blitz, the Corporation's art collection was homeless for 57 years – slightly longer than it had spent in its original building. After the planned rebuilding as part of Phase V was dropped, it seemed as if it would never have a home again, and that its paintings and sculptures were destined to remain a loan collection. But during the 1980s a handful of temporary exhibitions at Barbican Art Gallery and elsewhere offered the opportunity of displaying selected works for short periods, while additional curatorial, clerical and conservation staff were also appointed, the latter housed in studio and workshop space newly converted at Guildhall. The purchase of exhibits vote was greatly increased, and funding was provided for the rental of high security and environmentally controlled storage with Christie's Fine Art Security Services, in place of the former grubby ad hoc arrangements. It is against this optimistic background that the rebuilding of Guildhall Art Gallery has at last provided the permanent home which its originators and past supporters hoped for, purpose-built for the requirements of a modern Art Gallery and architecturally something of which the Corporation can indeed be extremely proud.